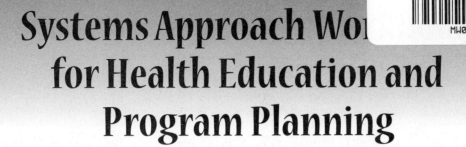

Systems Approach Workbook for Health Education and Program Planning

Mary E. Watson, MSCP, EdD

Associate Professor of Health Sciences

Northeastern University

Boston, Massachusetts

JONES & BARTLETT
LEARNING

World Headquarters

Jones & Bartlett Learning
40 Tall Pine Drive
Sudbury, MA 01776
978-443-5000
info@jblearning.com
www.jblearning.com

Jones & Bartlett Learning
Canada
6339 Ormindale Way
Mississauga, Ontario L5V 1J2
Canada

Jones & Bartlett Learning
International
Barb House, Barb Mews
London W6 7PA
United Kingdom

Jones & Bartlett Learning books and products are available through most bookstores and online booksellers. To contact Jones & Bartlett Learning directly, call 800-832-0034, fax 978-443-8000, or visit our website, www.jblearning.com.

Substantial discounts on bulk quantities of Jones & Bartlett Learning publications are available to corporations, professional associations, and other qualified organizations. For details and specific discount information, contact the special sales department at Jones & Bartlett Learning via the above contact information or send an email to specialsales@jblearning.com.

Production Credits

Publisher, Higher Education: Cathleen Sether
Acquisitions Editor: Shoshanna Goldberg
Senior Associate Editor: Amy L. Bloom
Senior Editorial Assistant: Kyle Hoover
Production Director: Amy Rose
Associate Production Editor: Julia Waugaman
Associate Marketing Manager: Jody Sullivan
V.P., Manufacturing and Inventory Control: Therese Connell
Composition: Cape Cod Compositors, Inc.
Cover Design: Kristin E. Parker
Cover Image: © javarman/ShutterStock, Inc.
Printing and Binding: Courier Stoughton
Cover Printing: Courier Stoughton

Library of Congress Cataloging-in-Publication Data
Watson, Mary E.
  Systems approach workbook for health education and program planning / Mary E. Watson.
      p. ; cm.
  Includes bibliographical references.
  ISBN-13: 978-0-7637-8660-1 (pbk., perforated)
  ISBN-10: 0-7637-8660-8 (pbk., perforated)
  1. Health education.   2. Health planning.   I. Title.
  [DNLM: 1. Health Education.   2. Program Evaluation.   3. Systems Analysis.
  4. Teaching—methods.   WA 18 W341s 2011]
  RA440.W38 2011
  613.071—dc22

                                                                          2010014833
6048

Printed in the United States of America
14 13 12 11 10   10 9 8 7 6 5 4 3 2 1

To Tom, my husband and best friend

and

To my dad, Edward Watson, whose work ethic I inherited.

CONTENTS

PREFACE

For the past 30 years I have been educating health professional students at the undergraduate and graduate levels. My experience includes teaching students who are preparing for the health professions to plan programs for a variety of settings, including patient education, staff development, clinical education, and for teaching their own health profession. I originally wrote a version of this workbook as a companion to the textbook used for the aforementioned classes. The textbooks I have used for the classes have changed over time, but the workbook has served a consistent purpose independent of the textbook.

The workbook serves to help students design a health planning program step-by-step, and to see the connections between the steps of the planning process. As students learn each part of program planning, the chapters of the workbook will help them to process the information, and ultimately to build their program. The workbook is designed to help students learn a systematic approach to program design that is logical and can be applied to many different settings. It is not meant to be a complete text on everything a program planner should know about this subject; it is, however, a way to begin to learn the basic and essential concepts about program design. Former students who used the original version of this workbook state that it served as their "bible." They have kept the workbook and continue to use it as a resource in their careers. They have also referred to it as a helpful "cookbook" when designing many different types of programs.

This updated version of the workbook has new features. The Mission Statement chapter is new, as is the chapter on Interventions and Behavioral Change Models. Three cases have been added and are referred to at the end of the chapters so students can work on theoretical cases for practice as they process the information. All of the chapters have been updated in content and references. The appendices contain new needs assessment and evaluation forms. The systems approach diagram has been modified to reflect each part of the program as a puzzle piece, emphasizing the point that puzzle pieces have to fit together to have complete and effective programs.

The Intended Audience

The audience for this workbook includes students planning careers as health educators, those planning careers in a specific health profession, and practicing professionals. The workbook will serve as a resource for people who have the responsibility to set up programs in a variety of settings such as non-profit organizations, schools, hospitals, or clinics.

ACKNOWLEDGMENTS

Credit is given to Charles W. Ford and Margaret K. Morgan for their influence on my early teaching. I also acknowledge my colleague, Professor Emeritus Thomas Barnes, with whom I co-taught program planning for several years. During that time, we constructed a systems approach diagram based on the work of Ford and Morgan. The diagram in this workbook represents my expanded thinking of that work. Appreciation to Zachary M. Hayes for drawing the systems approach illustration.

I want to give a special thank you to my colleague Annemarie Sullivan for her review of each chapter, for her contributions to the case studies that appear at the end of each chapter, and especially for the many program planning classes we have taught together. Her efforts in the classroom and collaborations on strategies for every class meeting have contributed to much of the thinking that went into this workbook.

I want to thank friends and colleagues for reading drafts of the chapters and for giving me valuable feedback. Thank you to Joan Harrington, and Professors Emeriti Lawrence Litwack, Tomas Harrington, and Gerald Schumacher.

A special thank you to Kyle Hoover, Senior Editorial Assistant, and Julia Waugaman, Associate Production Editor, who were always available when I had questions and encouraged me during the process of writing and editing each chapter; Shoshanna Goldberg, who first talked with me about doing this project, for her encouragement that this was a worthwhile endeavor; and to the students and colleagues who contributed to the Needs Assessment and Evaluation forms in the appendices. They are mentioned by name in those sections.

A special thank you to my husband, Tom Giancristiano, for his careful editing of numerous drafts and for his support during the many months that I worked on this project. I could not have done this project without him.

CHAPTER
1

Overview of a Systems Approach to Education and Program Planning

Chapter Objectives

- Discuss general system theory.
- Describe the various elements of general system theory.
- Briefly describe the components of a systems approach to education and program planning.
- List the combination of skills important for health promotion and for health care practitioners.
- Explain the advantages of a systems approach to program planning.
- Discuss some of the constraints that may impact the success of programs.

Introduction

The purpose of this chapter is to give an overview of system theory and then to show how systems thinking can be applied to health education and program planning.

An Overview of General System Theory

A. German biologist Ludwig von Bertalanffy was one of the first to propose the concept of *General System Theory* as far back as the 1940s.[1,2]

    1. System theory has been applied to math, science, research, technology, industry, education, policy, management, and organizations.

    2. It is a way to solve problems in that the whole system as well as the interaction between the parts is considered.

    3. Systems that are *open* interact with the world outside the system.[1(pp36–44)]

    4. A system as a whole works differently than the parts of a system; the whole is often greater than the sum of the parts.[3(pp11–12)]

    5. Principle: a system has functional identifiable parts that communicate efficiently and affect each other.[3(pp11–17)]

6. A system has several components, including: elements, interconnections, function or purpose (both tangible and intangible), and feedback.[2,3(pp11–17)]

Consider the following in applying these concepts to program planning:

- *Elements*—all of the tangible elements of the program would include all the people, facilities, materials, budget, mission, and participants. Examples of intangible elements would include morale, confidence in ability to succeed, the feeling people have about their work and working together, and whether they think the program is important.

- *Interconnections*—the relationships among the program parts that work together to result in achieving something. Consider how the budget, the people involved, the program materials, and the communication system all work toward a successful program.

- *Function and Purpose*—rationale, the reason behind the program or organization. There may be conflicting purposes between people involved or between different departments. When developing a program, it is important to be aware of these. Purposes may become clear through how people and the system behaves more than in the stated goals.[3(p14)]

- *Feedback*—the result of reviewing data and evaluative information and then using this to improve the system—in this case, the components of the program plan where needed. For example, program feedback can come from observing the participants during the process of the program, from informal and formal assessment of progress of the participants, or from the feedback from the organization and program personnel involved. The goal is to use the feedback to improve the program, resulting in a more successful outcome.

7. Systems thinking has been applied to health education and program planning[4–8] as well as to health professional education.[9–12] These are just a few examples; there are numerous other examples that can be found in literature or on the Internet.

A Systems Approach to Education and Program Planning

A. A systems approach provides a generalized logical approach to designing programs and units of instruction.

B. A systems approach is designed to emphasize the outcomes or competencies that participants will demonstrate.

C. Health education and health professional education may reflect a combination of skills related to:

1. *Cognitive domain* (knowledge)

2. *Psychomotor domain* (demonstration of skills)

3. *Affective domain* (attitudes and values)

D. A systems approach provides a process for considering the essential parts of the planning, implementation, and evaluation of single unit of instruction, a program, or an entire curriculum.

E. *System* implies an interconnectedness of the parts (refer to Systems Approach diagram in **Figure 1–1**). **Note:** The puzzle pieces are used to illustrate that the program planning parts fit together to form the whole. Information from formative and summative evaluation is feedback into the system parts and is used to make improvements to work toward a more successful program.

F. When evaluation results are not successful, each part of the system is reviewed to determine where adjustments are needed.

G. This system can be used for a variety of different types of program plans, including:

1. Community health education and promotion.

2. Patient education.

3. Work site health promotion.

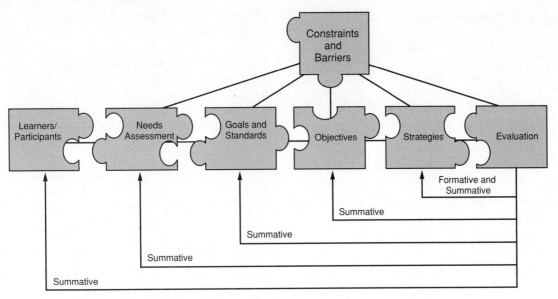

Figure 1-1   A systems approach to health education and program planning.
Source: © Mary E. Watson. Illustration by Zachary M. Hayes.

    4. Designing staff education.

    5. Clinical instruction for health professionals.

    6. Development of a single lesson, course, or a whole curriculum.

    7. Development of programs on a local, state, or national level.

H. Advantages of a systems approach include:

    1. Participants can identify the intent of the program.

    2. Learners know what they are expected to learn.

    3. Instructors know what they will be teaching.

    4. Knowledge, skills, and behaviors expected to change are identified.

    5. What learners can do at the end of instruction is documented.

    6. Provides a model for identifying problems so that steps can be taken for correction or improvement.

    7. Programs can be revised based on assessment and evaluation data.

    8. A program can be transferable in whole or in part, providing the new setting meets the needs of the program.

The Beginning of Instructional Design: The Learners/Participants

A. Consider that learners have specific needs, abilities, values, knowledge, skills, and learning styles.

B. The learners may be an individual, a group of people, or a community.

C. The learners are referred to as the priority population[4] or target population.[5–8]

D. Beginning the program planning process involves the following:

    1. Using a collaborative approach with the participants/community.

    2. Empowering participants even if in small ways.

    3. Giving participants/community choices whenever possible.

    4. Making participants an integral part of the program development and learning process.

Mission Statement

A. Is the first step of planning.

B. A statement that contains information about the overall direction and purpose of the program or organization.[4(p139),5(p31)]

C. Is broad enough to be adaptable yet has a focus.

D. May have a mission of the organization and then a program mission that fits into the larger mission.

E. Affects resource allocation, which depends on how well the program mission fits into the mission of the organization.

F. Should serve as a motivation for planners and participants.

Needs Assessment

A. Provides data that gives the program designer information to present relevant material and provide a program focus.

B. Provides justification for the program.

C. Can identify programs that are working well and where there are program needs or service gaps.[5(pp90–91)]

D. Considers the needs of the participant population whether they are individuals, a community, or a group.

E. Considers the physical, financial, and personnel resources needed of the program.

Goals and Standards

A. Goals are broad statements of direction and purpose.

B. Goals identify what is expected at the end of the program.

C. Goals will reflect the needs assessment and fit into the mission statement.

D. Goals provide guidance for the establishment of objectives and for ongoing planning and activities.

E. Goals are not directly measurable without evaluation criteria delineated.

F. Standards are the evaluative criteria for acceptable performance.

G. Standards determine whether or not the program was successful.

H. Standards may be equivalent to program or outcome objectives.

Objectives

A. Objectives are short-term, measurable, specific activities that include a time element.[5(p69),12(p62)]

B. Objectives work toward reaching the goals of the program.

C. Objectives address what is expected to change in the target population.

D. Different types of objectives are written for program planning to include administrative, learning, behavioral, impact, outcome, and environmental objectives.[4(p141–144)]

E. Learning objectives address the cognitive, psychomotor, and affective domains.

Interventional, Teaching, and Behavioral Change Strategies

A. These strategies are methods of teaching and activities designed to help the participant achieve the objectives and ultimately the goals.

B. Interventional strategies may include but are not limited to health communication, education, policy, environmental change, and community mobilization strategies.[4(pp202–216),8(pp87–89)]

C. A variety of teaching strategies should be designed to consider different learning styles and reading abilities.

D. Behavioral strategies are incorporated to help participants achieve behavioral change.

E. Alternative strategies are designed when evaluation indicates that participants are not achieving the objectives.

Evaluation

A. Evaluation is the method to determine if goals, standards, and objectives have been met.

B. Evaluation occurs during the program/course (formative). It is used to implement alternative strategies.

C. It occurs at the end of the program/course (summative).

D. Long-term follow-up evaluation is needed to determine the outcome after the program has been completed. These evaluative criteria are written as standards for evaluation.

E. Results are used to make changes where needed to accomplish more positive outcomes.
   1. Prerequisites reconsidered
   2. Program goals reviewed
   3. Objectives reconsidered
   4. New strategies introduced where needed
   5. Reliability and validity of evaluation procedures considered

Constraints or Barriers

A. Limitations that interfere with the learning process or with successful outcomes.

B. Can occur anywhere in the system.

C. Not always within control; however, recognize and limit them as much as possible.

D. Examples of constraints in each chapter.

Questions

The following questions are designed to help you process the information in this chapter and to understand how the parts of educational design fit together. You will be studying each part of the system separately in subsequent chapters. For now, study the diagram at the beginning of this chapter, note the connectivity of the parts, and consider the following:

1. Describe the components of systems thinking and how they are incorporated into the systems approach model.

2. Look at the evaluation system and the arrows referring back to each part. Describe how you think the evaluation results can be used to correct problems in the system.

3. Give an example from your background that illustrates how evaluation results were used (or could have been used) to correct a problem you or your classmates were having with a course.

4. What is the importance of requiring skills and competencies for the cognitive, psychomotor, and affective domains in preparing health professionals or in health promotion programs?

5. How do goals differ from objectives?

6. Describe how the mission statement may impact a program.

7. What might happen if a program designer does not do a needs assessment?

8. Consider a course or program that you have attended and describe all the different strategies that were used. What was the most helpful for you?

9. Recall a behavior you have tried to change. What strategies did or did not work in helping you achieve your goal?

10. Can you think of any constraints or barriers the academic calendar puts on programs that are using a goal-oriented/outcome-oriented approach? How might you address these constraints?

11. What are some examples from health education in the community that place constraints on a goal-oriented/outcome-oriented approach to program planning?

12. Write down any questions about the systems approach that you have at this point.

References

1. von Bertalanffy L. *General System Theory.* Rev. ed. New York, NY: George Braziller; 1968.
2. von Bertalanffy L, Wade, M, ed. *Theories Used in IS Research—General Systems Theory.* http://www.istheory.yorku.ca/generalsystemstheory.htm. Accessed March 21, 2010.
3. Meadows DH. *Thinking in Systems.* Wright D, ed. White River Junction, VT: Chelsea Green; 2008.
4. McKenzie JF, Neiger BL, Thackeray R. *Planning, Implementing, and Evaluating Health Promotion Programs.* San Francisco, CA: Pearson Education; 2009.
5. Timmreck TC. *Planning, Program Development, and Evaluation: A Handbook for Health Promotion, Aging, and Health Services.* Sudbury, MA: Jones and Bartlett; 2003.
6. Issel LM. *Health Program Planning and Evaluation—A Systematic Approach for Community Health.* Sudbury, MA: Jones and Bartlett; 2009.
7. Hodges BC. *Assessment and Planning in Health Programs.* Sudbury, MA: Jones and Bartlett; 2005.
8. Gilbert GG, Sawyer RG. *Health Education—Creating Strategies for School and Community Health.* 2nd ed. Sudbury, MA: Jones and Bartlett; 2000.
9. Shi L, Singh D. *Delivering Health Care in America: A Systems Approach.* 4th ed. Sudbury, MA: Jones and Bartlett; 2008.
10. *Healthy People 2010.* http://www.healthypeople.gov. Accessed March 21, 2010.
11. Ford CW, ed. *Clinical Education for the Allied Health Professions.* Saint Louis, MO: CV Mosby; 1978.
12. Ford CW, Morgan MK, eds. *Teaching in the Health Professions.* Saint Louis, MO: CV Mosby; 1976.

CHAPTER

2

Mission Statements

Chapter Objectives

- Describe the purpose of a mission statement.
- Develop criteria for creating a mission statement.
- Critique a variety of mission statements.
- Write a mission statement for your program planning projects.

Introduction

The purpose of this chapter is to help students develop meaningful mission statements for their programs. Planning begins with a mission statement that gives overall direction for a program. Most organizations will have a mission statement. A program may also have a mission statement, which will be consistent with that of the organization. Permission to do the program or a decision for funding may depend on how well the program mission is in line with the mission of the organization.

Definitions and Characteristics of a Mission Statement

A. Good planning begins with the mission statement.

B. A mission statement relates to what is important to the organization and what it wants to accomplish.

C. A mission statement is a statement that contains information about the overall direction and purpose of the program or organization.[1(pp139-140),2(pp31-33)]

D. A mission statement is an expression of the values and philosophy of the organization or program.[3(pp58-59)]

E. A mission statement is broad enough to be adaptable over time, yet has a focus.

F. A specific program mission will fit into the larger mission.

   1. The organization's mission statement is meant to work over time.

   2. The program's mission statement may only be appropriate for the time the program is running.

G. Often resource allocation depends on how well the program mission fits into the organization mission statement.

H. The mission statement sets the stage for developing program plans.

I. All programs should contribute to fulfilling the mission statement.

J. A mission statement should serve as a motivation for planners and participants.

Constraints or Barriers

A. Too many people want to incorporate their own agendas into the statement.

B. Mission statements become too long and unfocused to be meaningful.

C. The statement is not clear enough so it is left open to different interpretations.

D. A meaningless mission is soon forgotten.

E. Absence of a mission statement or a poorly developed one leaves people and programs without direction.

Examples of Mission Statements for Health-Related Organizations

Educational Institution

Be recognized as a leader in preparing health educators to make a difference in urban communities.

Program Mission Statements Consistent With the Institutional Mission

1. Be a model for incorporating urban experiential learning into the curriculum for health educators.

2. To promote collaborations with urban communities so there is a mutually beneficial relationship between the academic institution and the community.

Medical Center Mission Statement

Be known internationally for providing quality health care.

Program Mission Statement Consistent With the Medical Center

1. To promote cutting-edge research in all areas of medical practices affiliated with the medical center.

2. To promote preventative medicine in the care of all patients.

Community Health Education Center Mission Statement

Improve the lives of children through education, research, and innovative care.

Program Mission Statement Consistent With the Community Health Education Center Mission Statement

1. Conduct research on new asthma education materials to determine the impact on children.

2. Incorporate patient education in every aspect of care for children with diabetes.

What Comes Next?

The needs assessment, goals, and objectives that are consistent with the overall mission of the organization or program will be developed next.

Questions

The following questions are designed to help you process the information in this unit and to help you develop a mission statement for your program project. Please respond to the following:

1. Develop a list of criteria you believe to be important to use in writing a mission statement.

2. Search for 3 different mission statements either on the Internet or from organizations in which you are involved. These could include your college, place of employment, or where you have done clinical training. How well does the mission statement describe what you know about the organization? Describe how the mission fits into the criteria described in this chapter. What suggestions do you have for improving the mission statements?

3. When you have decided on a program-planning project to develop, check the organization's mission statement. Describe how well your project fits into the mission.

4. When you are satisfied that your program plan fits into the organization, write a mission statement for your program that is consistent with that of the organization.

Practice Cases

Consider the 3 cases described herein. Develop a mission statement that would be appropriate for the organization in each case and then one for each of the programs. Compare your mission statements with classmates or colleagues. Critique each statement using the criteria learned in this chapter. Decide which ones you like the best and why.

Case 1: Healthcare Clinic

You are an employee in a healthcare clinic. Your supervisor has asked you to create a program to decrease the risk of the H1N1 flu for all the clinic employees and for the clients who visit the clinic.

1. What would be a mission statement for the healthcare clinic?

2. What would be a program mission statement that would fit into the clinic mission statement?

Case 2: After School Program

You volunteer at an after school program for children in grades 3 through 5. Currently, they complete their homework, participate in craft projects, and have a snack. You think it might be a good idea to add physical activity and nutrition components to the existing program. Your supervisor agrees and asks you to develop a proposal.

1. What would be a mission statement for the after school program?

2. What would be a program mission statement that would fit into the mission of the after school program?

Case 3: Pharmacy

You are an intern at a local pharmacy. Many clients come in to ask questions about preventing the onset of certain diseases. You realize it would be a good idea to have a series of wellness lectures about obesity, diabetes, cardiovascular disease, and hypertension. Your supervisor says that this will be a great program for you to develop.

1. What would be a mission statement for the pharmacy?

2. What would be a wellness program mission statement that would fit into the mission of the pharmacy?

References

1. McKenzie JF, Neiger BL, Thackeray R. *Planning, Implementing, and Evaluating Health Promotion Programs.* San Francisco, CA: Pearson Education; 2009.
2. Timmreck TC. *Planning, Program Development, and Evaluation: A Handbook for Health Promotion, Aging, and Health Services.* Sudbury, MA: Jones and Bartlett; 2003.
3. Hodges BC. *Assessment and Planning in Health Programs.* Sudbury, MA: Jones and Bartlett; 2005.

3

Needs Assessment

Chapter Objectives

- Define the term *needs assessment*.
- Describe several purposes of performing a needs assessment.
- Develop survey instruments for a variety of needs assessments.
- Describe all the data sources used for needs assessment information.
- Identify sources of needs assessment information appropriate for your project.
- Design needs assessment instruments for your project.

Introduction

The purpose of this chapter is to provide students with a variety of ideas and strategies for performing a needs assessment. After reviewing the needs assessment possibilities, decide what is appropriate and what can reasonably be done for your project.

Definitions and Characteristics of a Needs Assessment

A. A systematic way to gather information about a problem or issue.

B. A process for identifying what already exists and what is missing in programs, gaps in services,[1(pp90–93)] or curriculum.

C. The process used to justify a program and identify resources needed for the program.

D. An essential part of a program plan. Program success will depend on performing a useful needs assessment and designing the program accordingly.

E. Serves as a foundation for developing the goals, objectives, strategies, and evaluation of the program plan.

F. Write goals and objectives for the needs assessment.[1(pp66–67)]

G. Sources of data:

1. Primary data—data directly collected from the population of concern (e.g., interviews, focus group, survey, nominal group process, observation)—has the advantage of being specific to the target group.[2(pp82–83),3(pp114–121)]

2. Secondary data—data already collected by someone else or an agency (e.g., data from government agencies, review of the literature, statistics from existing records)—has the advantage of being available but may not be completely applicable to the population.[2(pp94–97),3(pp114–117)]

H. Identifying resources needed to plan and implement the program.

1. Personnel resources—Who will work on the project? What will their roles be? Will there be committees and subcommittees set up?

2. Financial resources—What are the funding sources? Consider needs for planning, implementation, and evaluation. Where will limited funding best be spent?

3. Physical resources—Where will the program take place? Will the physical facilities and geographic location meet the needs of the audience/targeted population?

I. Through the needs assessment, the program planner gathers information to:

1. Consider the specific interests of the target population (learners/patients/community/group).

2. Identify or gather more information about a problem that has been identified or previously documented.

3. Provide a specific focus for program planning.

4. Assure that the program plans and materials used are relevant.

5. Determine if the need is for programming or other noneducational interventions.

6. Consider the resource needs of the program to assure that the plans can be carried out.

7. Identify specific skills and competencies needed for the targeted population to change behavior.

8. Identify strategies that will affect attendance and participation of the audience or target population.

Performing a Needs Assessment

A. The type of needs assessments performed will depend on the type of program/unit of instruction being planned.

B. Some are time consuming and costly. For example:

1. Large-scale assessments of community healthcare needs.

2. Use of data about the target population that already exists to decrease time and funds for large-scale assessments.

C. Some are as simple as a short questionnaire. For example:

1. Survey of a college class to determine the needs of students in a course.

2. Ask participants what is important to them and what will make a positive experience for them.

3. Ask target group what they would like to see changed or implemented.

D. Examples of strategies used to gather needs assessment information that will be covered in this chapter are as follows:

1. Surveys and questionnaires

2. Gathering information on the needs of participants

3. Review of the literature, statistics, and health data

4. Focus groups

5. Community forums or town meetings

6. Nominal group process (consensus conference)

7. Information from professional groups

8. Sources of patient education information
9. Observations
10. Interviews

Surveys and Questionnaires

A. These are tools that systematically gather data about individuals, groups, or organizations. The process includes:

1. Consideration of how much funding is available for doing the survey.
2. Choosing the appropriate target group or individuals to survey.
3. Designing or choosing the survey so that it gives you the information needed.
4. Deciding how the survey will be administered (in person, mail, electronically).
5. Determination of who will do personal administration (if applicable) and how they will be trained so that the data gathered is reliable.

B. Surveys can be as brief as 1 page or less or can be longer in length. Appendix A has sample survey instruments.

C. Whatever the survey length, consider the following criteria:

1. The questions should be straightforward and as uncomplicated as possible.
2. Be sure to ask exactly the questions that you intend to ask.
3. Select key issues in which to focus.
4. Arrange the questions/items in a logical sequence.
5. If a scale is used, assign a descriptor to each number.
6. Instruments should be easy to administer and score.
7. Provide spaces for comments either after each question or at the end of the survey.
8. Choose participants who have the information you are seeking.

D. Test the instrument.

1. Have colleagues review.
2. Do a sample group first, if possible.

E. Examples of questions to ask:

1. What are your topics of interest?
2. What do you want to learn?
3. What are your current health practices?
4. What do you want to change?
5. What needs are you trying to meet?

F. You may have to survey people at a variety of levels.

1. Workers and management may want something different; therefore, one may have to negotiate program plans accordingly.
2. For example: While planning an employee fitness center, the following could occur:
   - Employees want equipment and hours of operation that significantly differ from what management envisioned.
   - Program designer would need to consider that success of the fitness facility depends on meeting the needs of both groups.
   - Resources may not be allocated from management unless these issues are negotiated.
   - Employees may not use the facility if it does not meet their needs.

Gathering Information on the Needs of Participants

When developing a program where people will come together as a group, there are many considerations important for success. A quality program may not be successful if these issues are not addressed in the planning process. (Some of this information will be known and some of it will need to be asked in a survey of the specific group.)

A. Geographic location and logistics

    1. Where is the group to meet?

    2. Is it convenient to the target population?

    3. Is parking available or accessible to public transportation?

    4. Is it necessary to provide transportation?

    5. What will be the best time to offer the program that will meet the needs of the target group?

B. Socioeconomic information

    1. Who is the target group?

    2. Is the program affordable for the intended group?

    3. Will the target group perceive the cost/benefit to be worthwhile?

C. Language, culture, and disabilities

    1. What is the primary language of the target group?

    2. Is a translator needed?

    3. Are provisions needed for hearing-impaired participants?

    4. Are provisions needed for physically disabled participants?

    5. Are materials designed to be culturally appropriate?

D. Age of participants

    1. Need age-appropriate materials and examples to present.

    2. Learners want practical information; they want to know how the information will be used and how information can be related to previous experiences.

    3. Would it be useful to provide child care to make it easier for parents to attend?

E. Education and prerequisites

    1. Do all participants have the background for the program material?

    2. What prerequisite knowledge is needed as a base?

    3. Have learners retained prerequisite knowledge?

    4. Assure that materials are prepared at the appropriate reading levels.

F. Professional background or previous experience

    1. Have participants been working in a profession or related field?

    2. What is their practical experience?

    3. Connect new information to previous experiences whenever possible.

G. What they already know

    1. What are the competencies or skills of the participants?

    2. Do they have any flawed learning that needs to be undone or misunderstandings that need to be corrected?

    3. What are the gaps in competencies and skills?

H. Materials needed to teach the class or program

    1. A syllabus that includes the goals, objectives, strategies, and the intended outcomes that the participants can expect from the program.

2. Strategies and materials for different learning styles.

3. Physical facilities (appropriate size and location of room, whiteboard, setup of the room that is conducive for the planned activities, etc).

4. A pretest or questionnaire for the group (see sample surveys in Appendix A).

Review of the Literature, Statistics, and Health Data

A. Use a review of the literature.

   1. Data about the problem.

   2. Learn what has been done already to solve the problem.

   3. Learn from the success and failures of others.

B. Program statistics can be a useful part of the needs assessment. Examples:

   1. Only 60% of the students in the class passed the final examination. In reviewing this data, ask questions such as:

      • Did they have the prerequisite knowledge needed?

      • Were there strategies to meet different learning styles?

      • Was the exam objective, reliable, and valid?

      • Were there any controllable factors outside the class that interfered with participant success?

   2. A morning fitness program for elders attracted 20 participants for the first session. Only 30% came to the second session. In reviewing this data, ask questions such as:

      • Was the time and location meeting their needs?

      • Was the pace of the session appropriate for the participants?

      • Were the participants asked about their expectations and what they wanted from the program?

      • Did the instructor attend to the needs of the participants during the session?

      • Did the participants have the affective and psychomotor skills needed for success in the program?

   3. In both of the previous examples, use information to determine the specific problem to be addressed and make changes to improve the success of the participants and program.

C. Using health data—Example:

   1. Data indicating that 12% of students in a school suffer from asthma-related symptoms.

   2. Use questions as a base for deciding what other strategies are needed to gather more information about the health problem.

      • What related issues need to be addressed (such as policies, environmental issues, and education)?

      • What programs would be helpful, and who should be involved?

      • What do teachers, the children with asthma, and classmates need to know?

      • How should the parents be involved in the program?

Focus Groups

Focus groups bring together a relatively small group of people who are asked to respond to new ideas or to solicit their views on an issue or service. Focus groups utilize a form of brainstorming.[1(p98),2(p89),4(p14)]

A. A summary of the process is[1(p98),2(p89),4(p14)]:
 1. Identify approximately 8–12 invited people who have information or a point of view about the issue.
 2. Several focus groups are often conducted with different participants using the same questions.
 3. Those invited should represent the target population.
 4. Sometimes an incentive will encourage participation.
 5. Questions are prepared ahead of time and a facilitator is identified to lead the group.
 6. The facilitator asks each question and solicits responses from the participants and sometimes asks the participants to prioritize the responses.
 7. Care is taken during the session so that:
     • One person does not dominate the group.
     • Everyone has a chance to give input.
     • The facilitator does not lead the group in the direction of a certain viewpoint.
     • Judgments are not made during the session.
     • The facilitator recognizes cues indicating something needs to be followed up on that was not part of the scripted questions.
 8. The session is recorded and/or videotaped.
 9. The session is transcribed and the responses analyzed.
     • Issues and themes delineated.
     • Potential solutions described.
     • Services needed identified.
 10. Analysis is reviewed by the program planners.
B. Examples of potential topics for focus groups include:
 1. Determining the most pressing healthcare issues in a community.
 2. Determining current health practices and beliefs of a group.
 3. Acquiring feedback on a draft program plan.
 4. Soliciting ideas on how to improve established protocols in a healthcare facility or community.

Community Forums or Town Meetings

The strategy brings together people from the target population to get their views on how they see the community needs.[2(p88)] These forums are advertised so that anyone in the community can attend[1(pp94–95),2(pp88–89)] (as opposed to people being invited to a focus group).

A. Who attends[1(pp93–95)]:
 1. Community leaders from key organizations
 2. Members of the target population who know about the issues
 3. Interested professionals and other community members concerned with the issues
B. A summary of the process is[1(pp94–95),2(pp88–89)]:
 1. The facilitator explains the purpose of the meeting.
 2. The facilitator presents key questions or concerns to the audience.
 3. Responses of the audience are taken on each question or concern.
 4. Designated recorders take down information or record the sessions.
 5. The group can use the brainstorming approach.
 6. Facilitators could solicit responses in writing as well as through questionnaires.
 7. Information is reviewed by interested parties or program planners.

C. Examples of potential community forums for college students:
  1. In a college setting, bring student government leaders, club leaders, and members of the student body together to discuss current health needs of students.
  2. Bring administrators, faculty, and students together to hear views on a new campus physical fitness facility being planned.

D. Example of a community forum at an elder housing center:
  1. Bring together residents and staff to discuss plans for health and fitness classes.
  2. Bring together residents and staff to discuss needs for monthly programming on their most pressing health issues.

Nominal Group Technique

A. A structured process to gain consensus from a group of stakeholders who have the information needed to be knowledgeable participants.[2(p88)] They are invited participants and are representatives of the priority population.[2(pp89–90),5]

B. A summary of the process is[2(pp89–90),5]:
  1. Five to seven people are invited to the group (several groups may be meeting concurrently).
  2. They are asked to respond to a question in writing without discussing.
  3. They then share responses using a round-robin method.
  4. Each idea is exactly recorded (whiteboard or large sticky notes).
  5. These are made visible for all to see during the session.
  6. Responses are discussed among everyone and clarified.
  7. The participants are asked to rank order the responses privately.
    • Votes are tallied to determine what is rated the highest by the group.
    • The most important 5 items are identified and each one is written on an index card.
    • Each person then ranks the 5 highest priorities (using 5 as the highest rank and 1 as the lowest).
    • Each idea is given a number based on the tally from the total votes for that item.
    • The highest rated ideas are the ones most favored or important to the group.
  8. This process can be done with several nominal groups of 5–7 people going on at the same time, with the tallies from each group put together for a final total.
  9. Examples of issues for a nominal group could be:
    • To determine future direction of a profession (participants might include people from academic institutions, accreditation agencies, researchers and practitioners, and public representatives).
    • To determine community priorities of health issues (participants might include community leaders, representatives from a variety of health professional groups, and public representatives).

Information from Professional Groups

A. Information can be used in planning programs to meet the needs of professional groups.
  1. What are the current and future needs of the profession?
  2. What is the mission/philosophy of the profession?
  3. In what direction is the profession headed?

B. What are the needs of the practicing professionals?

C. What are the criteria for licensing or registration in the profession?

    1. What are the criteria for renewal of one's professional license?

    2. What programs would meet continuing education requirements?

    3. What is the process to approve a program for continuing education credit?

Sources of Patient Education Information

Sources of patient education information can include the following[6]:

A. Data from the literature or from professional experience such as:

    1. Who is most likely to develop specific complications?

    2. Who is at risk for developing health problems?

B. Demographic information from:

    1. Patient charts and medical records

    2. Data from patient and family

C. Health department documents about the priority population:

    1. Morbidity and mortality statistics

    2. Epidemiology data

D. What teaching was done and what competencies did the patient master?

    1. Preoperative teaching such as coughing techniques, breathing techniques, and breathing devices to be used postoperatively.

    2. In asthma education—has the client mastered the use of a peak flow meter?

    3. In diabetic education—has the client mastered the skill of monitoring blood insulin levels?

E. What is it that the client/patient wants to achieve?

    1. What is really important to the individual?

    2. What is important for the family to learn so they can be supportive?

F. Consider age, educational background, and language competence.

G. What knowledge, skills, values, and attitudes does the patient have?

    1. What are previous health practices?

    2. Has the client who is in a cardiac rehabilitation program already adopted a lifestyle that includes exercise?

    3. Does the client perceive that the information is important?

    4. Does the client have the psychomotor skills needed to perform?

H. Assess what the patient/client already knows and needs to know.

I. Are there any faulty learning or barriers that need to be corrected?

J. What knowledge, skills, and attitudes will need to be reinforced?

Observations

A. Observation can provide information about the people and the environment. Observers must be trained in the process so that data collected is reliable.

    1. Direct observation—observing the situation, behavior, or people directly.[2(pp90–91)] For example:

       • Observing how children with asthma use their inhaler during physical activities.

- Observing bike riders for use of helmets and other behaviors that keep them safe.
- Observing the types of food that children choose in the school cafeteria.

2. Indirect observation—observing the results or outcomes of a behavior or by asking others.[2(pp90–91)] For example:
   - Asking parents about the behaviors of their child with asthma.
   - Observing the results of flossing and brushing teeth during a dental checkup.
   - Asking adult children about the adherence to medication of an elder parent.

B. Information from the observation is reviewed and:
  1. Problems that need to be addressed are identified.
  2. Factors that contribute to the problem are documented.
  3. Problems in prior learning are identified.
  4. Knowledge, skills, and/or attitudes that need to be developed or reinforced are identified.
  5. It allows one to consider what is most significant to address in the program.

Interviews

A. May be with an individual or a group.

B. May be the first step in gathering data to be followed by using the information to develop another means of assessment.

C. May supplement other forms of data to verify information collected in other ways.

D. Useful in obtaining data from individuals who do not express themselves well on a written survey.

E. Can gather information important in identifying and solving problems—for example:
  1. Does an individual recognize that a problem exists?
  2. How does the individual perceive the problem?
  3. Does the individual have any ideas for improvements or solutions?
  4. What does the individual like the most and the least about a situation or program?
  5. What is going well and not so well?
  6. What is important to the individual?
  7. What are his or her interests, goals, and hopes for the program in the future?

F. Advantages of interviews:
  1. Nonverbal communication can be observed.
  2. Expectations and assumptions can be clarified.
  3. Positive rapport can begin to develop.

G. Appropriate timing is essential—for example:
  1. Interviewing someone during crisis may not result in reliable data.
  2. Interviews done when a problem has just been discovered may result in relevant information being shared that may be forgotten later. Example: A critical incident occurs at a work site. Interviewing those who were there at the time is better done soon after the incident.

Self-Assessments

A. Self-assessments are done by gathering data directly from the target group that gives the program planner information about the group's risk factors and health behaviors.

B. Self-assessments may be used to help participants evaluate what is important to them and what they would like to change.

C. Health risk appraisals can be used as a self-assessment as a means to motivate people—done through a questionnaire.[2(pp91–92)]

    1. Questions might be about health behavior, personal or family health history, demographics, and physical data.

    2. The results generate individual and group reports.

    3. Planners can use the individual reports or group reports depending on the program plan.

D. Self-evaluations can be done in a questionnaire or individual interview.

    1. Help participants assess their own behavior.

    2. What do they want to change?

    3. What is important to them?

    4. Help participants assess their level of commitment in making a plan to change.

Constraints Related to Needs Assessments

A. Financial resources may limit the scope and scale of the assessment.

B. There is an unknown degree of certainty that the population has the information.

C. There is an unsatisfactory degree to which the population realizes what they need. For example:

    1. Healthcare practitioners may not be interested in attending a seminar about a new procedure, but they will need the information to perform their job in the future.

    2. Students may not be interested in a particular course in the curriculum, although there is a need to acquire the skills covered in the course.

    3. Children may not see the need for bicycle safety education.

D. In the cases such as just described, it is important to help the participants understand why the information is necessary. Affective domain objectives and strategies to develop attitudes and values are helpful to consider in these situations.

Note: Please refer to Appendix A for sample needs assessment instruments.

Questions

After reading this chapter on needs assessments, respond to the following questions:

1. Consider a project you would like to develop. What will be the specific purposes of the needs assessment for the project you have chosen?

2. What sources of information will be necessary to gather for your needs assessment?

3. What types of needs assessment instruments will you develop, and what processes will you go through to gather the information? List all that you consider to be important in your ideal world and then designate what is practical to do. (See Appendix A for sample instruments.)

4. Describe any compromises that you are making in doing only what is practical. If so, are there any ways to decrease the compromises to assure that you have the most accurate and useful information?

5. Write down any questions you have about developing and performing a needs assessment.

Practice Cases

Consider again the three cases that you worked on in Chapter 2. Answer the questions for each case. Then discuss your answers with other students in your class or with colleagues. Compare your answers and write down what you consider the most useful list of responses.

Case 1: Healthcare Clinic

You are an employee in a healthcare clinic. Your supervisor has asked you to create a program to decrease the risk of H1N1 flu in current employees and patients who visit the clinic.

1. Who should be involved in the planning process and why?

2. What strategies will you use to determine the needs of the healthcare providers and for the patients?

3. How would you determine what current polices relate to this problem?

4. What needs assessment strategies would you use to find out if the polices are working and if they are being adhered to by the employees?

5. Indicate which strategies are examples of primary data collection and which are secondary data collection.

6. Is there anything else you want to say about the needs assessment in this case that was not asked about in the previous questions?

Case 2: After School Program

You volunteer at an after school program for children in grades 3 through 5. Currently, they complete their homework, participate in craft projects, and have a snack. You think it might be a good idea to add a physical activity component and a nutrition component to the existing program. Your supervisor agrees and asks you to develop a proposal for this.

1. Who should be involved in the planning process and why?

2. What strategies will you use to determine the needs of the children?

3. What types of data are you interested in collecting, and how will you go about collecting it?

4. How would you determine what current polices relate to the program you want to develop?

5. Indicate which of your needs assessment strategies are examples of primary data collection and which ones are secondary data collection.

6. Is there anything else you want to say about the needs assessment in this case that was not asked about in the previous questions?

Case 3: Pharmacy

You are an intern at a local pharmacy. Many clients come in to ask questions of the pharmacists about preventing the onset of certain diseases. You believe it would be a good idea to have a series of wellness lectures about obesity, diabetes, cardiovascular disease, and hypertension. Your supervisor says that this will be a great program for you to develop.

1. Who should be involved in the planning process and why?

2. What strategies will you use to determine the needs of the target participants?

3. What types of data are you interested in collecting, and how will you go about collecting it?

4. How would you determine what current polices relate to the program you want to develop?

5. Indicate which of your needs assessment strategies are examples of primary data collection and which ones are secondary data collection.

6. Is there anything else you want to say about the needs assessment in this case that was not asked about in the previous questions?

References

1. Timmrek TC. *Planning, Program Development, and Evaluation. A Handbook for Health Promotion, Aging & Health Service.* Sudbury, MA: Jones and Bartlett; 2003.
2. McKenzie JF, Neiger BL, Smeltzer JL. *Planning, Implementing, and Evaluating Health Promotion Programs.* San Francisco, CA: Pearson Education, Inc; 2009.

3. Hodges BC. *Assessment and Planning in Health Programs.* Sudbury, MA: Jones and Bartlett; 2005.
4. Gilbert GG, Sawyer RG. *Health Education—Creating Strategies for School and Community Health.* 2nd ed. Sudbury, MA: Jones and Bartlett; 2000.
5. Centers for Disease Control and Prevention. *Evaluation Briefs, Gaining Consensus Among Stakeholders through Nominal Group Technique.* 2006. http://www.cdc.gov/healthyyouth/evaluation/pdf/brief7.pdf. Accessed March 15, 2010.
6. Watson M. A systems approach to patient education. In: Litwack K, *A Core Curriculum for Post Anesthesia Nursing.* 4th ed. Philadelphia, PA: WB Saunders; 1999.

CHAPTER
4

Developing Goals and Standards

Chapter Objectives

- Define the characteristics of goal statements.
- Describe the purpose of writing standards related to goal statements.
- Identify sources from where goals are derived.
- Write goals and standards for different types of program plans.
- Develop goals and standards for your program project.

Introduction

There is a variety of different styles for writing program goals. The style presented in this workbook will use the format of writing a goal and then standards for evaluation under each goal. In this format, the goal is a simple statement of direction with the standards providing criteria for evaluation. This is an efficient format to use since there may be several standards written for one goal. The goal is written just once and the standards qualify the goal.

Definitions and Characteristics of Goal Statements

The following are definitions and characteristics of goal statements[1(pp65–82),2(pp48–55),3(p21)]:

A. Broad statements of direction.

B. General statements of learning outcomes or program directions.

C. General knowledge, skills, or attitudes that the learner/participant will have after the instruction takes place.

D. Provides guidance for the establishment of objectives.

E. Provides guidance for directing the planning activities and strategies in the program plan.

Examples of Goal Statements

A. The elderly participants will be able to function independently.

B. To graduate competent health educators.

C. To develop a program for cardiac risk factor modification for people in the community.

D. To educate participants in developing heart-healthy meals.

E. To increase the number of participants using the fitness center.

Standards Are Written Related to the Goals

A. Standards are criteria for acceptable performance.

B. Standards are the criteria for determining if the program goals were successful.

C. Standards often represent the ultimate program outcome.

Examples of Standards Related to the Goals

A. **Goal:** The elderly participants will be able to function independently.

Standard: On a follow-up survey 4 months after the program, 95% of the participants will report that they can prepare their own small meals.

Standard: On a follow-up survey 4 months after the program, 95% of the participants will report that they can do light housekeeping around their home.

B. **Goal:** To graduate competent health educators.

Standard: One year postgraduation, all students who take the Certified Health Education Specialist exam will receive a passing score.

Standard: One year postgraduation, employer surveys will rate health program graduates hired as above average in each category.

C. **Goal:** To develop a program for cardiac risk factor modification for people in the community.

Standard: At the end of the program, participants will document their specific plan for decreasing their cardiac risk factors.

Standard: On a 3-month follow-up survey, the program participants will report that they have been successful in decreasing at least 1 cardiac risk factor.

D. **Goal:** To educate participants in developing heart-healthy meals.

Standard: On the last day of the program, participants will share with the class 3 heart-healthy meal plans they have developed.

Standard: Three months after the program, participants will report that they have been successful in continuing to develop heart-healthy meal plans.

E. **Goal:** To increase the number of participants using the fitness center.

Standard: One month after the changes are made in the fitness center schedule of open times, there will be 100 participants using the center each day.

Standard: One month after physical changes are made in the fitness center, a survey of participants will indicate they are satisfied with the changes.

What to do with results: When the standard is not met in the evaluation, each part of the system is examined to determine what changes need to be made for more successful results.

Developing Goals for Patient Care

When developing goals for patient care, keep the following in mind[2(pp45–55)]:

A. Teaching patients requires some special considerations.

B. General goals and purposes of patient teaching include:

1. To provide information that will help improve the outcome of their health issue. For example:

   • Help patients understand their diagnosis.

   • To assist patients to care for themselves.

   • To help patients learn ways to prevent a relapse of their problem.

2. To teach skills needed to perform activities. For example:
   - How to use an oxygen cylinder safely.
   - How to floss teeth correctly.
   - How to use exercise equipment safely and effectively.
   - How to use a walker to get around the house.
3. Special considerations for patient teaching.
   - Keep the patient as involved as possible in his or her own care.
   - Keep the focus on the highest quality of life for the patient.
   - Involve family—consider the role of significant others in care.
   - Reinforce what is already known to the patient.
   - Explain procedures, any follow-up needed, and information about medications.
   - Consider different learning styles when teaching.
   - Give writing materials to the patient to use as you explain and then check his or her level of understanding.
   - Have written materials available to give to the patient.
   - Discuss the future—what happens after discharge.
   - Advise about home health follow-up and ways to manage at home.
   - Provide telephone numbers that the patient may need if any questions arise later.
   - Help the patient self-evaluate what he or she knows and what questions he or she has.

From Where Are Goals Derived?

A. Results of needs assessments. For example:
   1. Statistics indicating risk for specific health problems.
   2. Statistics indicating increased incidence of specific diseases.
   3. Goals and directions that are desired by the participants.
B. From the healthcare team.
   1. All health professionals involved with patient care.
   2. The patient and family members as appropriate.
C. Mission statements of the facility, organization, or unit.
D. Philosophy of the unit/healthcare facility or corporation.
E. Professional guidelines for standards of care.
F. Healthcare facility/unit procedures for care.
G. Accreditation agency essentials and guidelines.
H. Community needs.
I. Licensing boards.
J. Boards that write professional exams.
K. Competencies for professional practice.
   1. Scope of practice identified by the profession.
   2. Statements of competence.
   3. Content outlined in task delineations.
   4. Levels of professional practice, for example:
      - Physical therapist (PT) vs. physical therapy assistant (PTA).
      - Physicians (MD) vs. physician assistants (PAs).

- Certified respiratory therapy technician (CRTT) vs. registered respiratory therapist (RRT).
- Medical laboratory technician (MLT) vs. medical technologist (MT).

L. Direct observation. For example:

   1. Observing a high error rate in documenting patient treatments.

   2. Observing errors in the use of new equipment.

M. Review of records/critical incidents.

N. Problems noted during a task analysis.

O. The purchase of new equipment or the implementation of a new procedure.

P. Any problem identified by some other means.

Goal Development Followed by Needs Assessment

Sometimes goals are developed first or implied by the nature of the task, and then a needs assessment follows. For example:

A. To decrease the incidence of postoperative complications in surgical patients.

B. To increase patient adherence with prescribed medications.

C. Goals for a specific course that is part of a curriculum.

Needs Assessment Leads to Goal Development

Other times, a needs assessment will be done first and will indicate the goals to be developed. For example:

A. To implement health education programs to meet the needs of the community.

B. To implement a new health professional program.

C. To develop programs for staff recertification or for continuing education.

Constraints or Barriers

A. You may not have the physical or financial resources to achieve the goals and standards to the ideal level.

B. Time constraints may result in some participants not achieving all the goals of a course or program.

C. Participants may not have developed the attitudes and values needed for accomplishing the goals of a program.

D. The purpose of identifying these problems is to have the information needed to limit the constraints or barriers where possible, so that the greatest number of participants can be successful in achieving the goals.

Questions

The following questions are designed to help you process the information in this chapter and help you develop goals and standards for your project.

1. Consider the following goals and write 2 standards for each one.

   Goal No. 1: Participants will be able to manage their own asthma.

   Standard:

   Standard:

Goal No. 2: Participants will value a healthy lifestyle.

Standard:

Standard:

Goal No. 3: To improve healthy choices in the school cafeteria.

Standard:

Standard:

2. Consider a program that you might like to implement and the goals that would apply.

Program:

Goal No. 1:

Goal No. 2:

3. Write a standard of acceptable performance for each of your goals.

Standard for goal No. 1:

Standard for goal No. 2:

4. Conduct a self-evaluation of goals and standards by responding to following:

   A. Describe how each of your goals meets the description under "Definitions and Characteristics of Goal Statements" in this chapter.

   B. Describe how your standards will determine program success or how they indicate the criteria for acceptable performance.

Note: If your standards are not written in a way that indicates the criteria for acceptable performance or program success, review the chapter information and then rewrite the standards.

5. Given your profession (or work situation):

   A. Make a list of where program goals might be derived.

   B. Write down 3 ideas for programs related to your work or future career plans that would be useful to develop.

6. How would you rate your ability to write goals and standards?

7. Write down any questions that you have related to this chapter.

Practice Cases

Here are the 3 cases you worked on in the previous 2 chapters. Write a goal and 2 standards for each goal. Compare with your classmates and work together to evaluate how well the goals and standards meet the criteria learned in this chapter.

Case 1: Healthcare Clinic

You are an employee in a healthcare clinic. Your supervisor has asked you to create a program to decrease the risk of H1N1 flu in current employees and patients who visit the clinic.

   Goal:

   Standard:

   Standard:

Case 2: After School Program

You volunteer at an after school program for children in grades 3 through 5. Currently, they complete their homework, participate in craft projects, and have a snack. You think it might be a good idea to add physical activity and a nutrition component to the existing program. Your supervisor agrees and asks you to develop a proposal for this.

Goal:

Standard:

Standard:

Case 3: Pharmacy

You are an intern at a local pharmacy. Many clients come in to ask questions of the pharmacists about preventing the onset of certain diseases. You realize it would be a good idea to have a series of wellness lectures about obesity, diabetes, cardiovascular disease, and hypertension. Your supervisor says that this will be a great program for you to develop.

Goal:

Standard:

Standard:

References

1. Timmreck TC. *Planning, Program Development, and Evaluation. A Handbook for Health Promotion, Aging and Health Services.* Sudbury, MA: Jones and Bartlett; 2003.
2. Watson ME. A systems approach to patient education. In: Litwack, K, ed. *A Core Curriculum for Post Anesthesia Nursing.* 4th ed. Philadelphia, PA: WB Saunders; 1999.
3. Gilbert GG, Sawyer RG. *Health Education—Creating Strategies for School and Community Health.* 2nd ed. Sudbury, MA: Jones and Bartlett; 2000.

CHAPTER
5
Writing Objectives

Chapter Objectives

- Differentiate between different types of objectives used in program planning.
- Describe how objectives differ from goal statements.
- Define the 3 domains of learning.
- Distinguish between general and specific objectives.
- Recognize common errors that occur in writing objectives.
- Write objectives for all levels in the cognitive, psychomotor, and affective domains.
- Write objectives that are appropriate for your program planning project.

Introduction

There are several different types of objectives used in program planning. They are used for different purposes during the planning and implementation of a program. Objectives all work toward achieving the program goals. Terminology can be confusing since sometimes there is more than 1 term used to describe the same type of objective. An overview of definitions is presented first to help with the understanding of terminology used for objectives. Then examples are given to illustrate how to write each type of objective.

Part 1—An Overview of Definitions

A. Definition of objectives[1(pp68–84),2(pp21–26)]

    1. A statement that is short term, specific, and measurable.

    Note: This is compared to goals that are generally stated.

    2. Activity having a timeline for completion.

    3. Action oriented and works toward meeting the goals of a program.

    4. Describes what the participants will know and be able do after the experience (course, seminar, program).

5. Provides direction for instruction and assessment.

6. Needed to evaluate knowledge, skills, attitude, and behavior change.

7. May be written for several different parts of the program such as the needs assessment, the administrative tasks, and for teaching the program.

B. Administrative objectives (other terms used are *process objectives*, *program development objectives*, and *planning objectives*).

   1. Written in terms of all the tasks, activities, and plans that will result in the accomplishment of the program.[3(pp29–30)]

   2. Focus on all the things that are needed to carry out the program; i.e., resources (personnel, materials, funds, space), activities to be developed, participant recruitment, attendance, data collection techniques, etc.[4(pp142–147)]

   3. Example of a goal for the 2 objectives that follow:

   To provide diabetic education in all community health centers.

   - Example 1 of an administrative planning objective:

     The health educator will recruit 6 clients at each community health center to participate in the diabetic education program offered monthly.

     Note: What makes this a complete objective is that it specifies *who* (the health educator), *action* (will recruit clients for the program), *criterion/standards* (6 at each community health center), and *for what purpose* (to participate in a diabetic education program).

   - Example 2 of an administrative planning objective:

     The health educator (*who*) will teach (*action*) a diabetic education session (*what*) in the community health centers (*conditions*) 1 day per month for 6 patients for the next year (*criterion/standards*).

C. General objectives (or general instructional objectives)[2(p21),5]

   1. An outcome of instruction that is stated in general terms.

   2. Provides broad guidelines for instructional direction.

   3. Needs to be further defined by specific learning outcomes to clarify the intent and to evaluate performance.

   4. Uses abstract verbs such as *appreciates*, *understands*, *knows*.

   5. Often many specific objectives written for each general objective.

   6. May stand as a goal with the specific objectives indicating the measurable aspect.[1(p70)]

   7. Example of a general instructional objective: Understands the food pyramid.

   Note: This could also be considered a goal for a unit of instruction within a larger, more comprehensive program goal such as:

   To provide a comprehensive nutrition program to students in grade 6.

D. Specific learning outcomes (other terms are *learning objectives*, *specific objectives*, *performance objectives*, *behavioral objectives*, and *measurable objectives*).

   1. These are the intended outcomes stated in terms of *specific*, *observable*, and *measurable* participant performance.

   2. They state behaviors that the students will engage in to indicate they have achieved the general objective.

   3. They represent what the instructor expects to observe when the student understands.

   4. They use specific action verbs that can be evaluated, such as *label*, *choose*, and *create*.

   5. Examples of specific learning objectives for the general objective:

      1.0 Understand the food pyramid. (general)

         1.1 Label the major categories in the food pyramid. (specific)

1.2　Given a picture of a food, choose where it would go in the food pyramid. (specific)

　　1.3　Create a daily menu using the food pyramid. (specific)

These objectives work toward the program goal:

To provide a comprehensive nutrition program to students in grade 6.

6. Note the numbering system used when writing general and specific objectives.

- 1.0 used for the general objective

- 1.1, 1.2, 1.3 for the specific objectives.

- The next general objective for this unit of instruction would be 2.0 and would be followed by 2.1, 2.2, etc., for the specific objectives.

E. Behavioral Objectives. In the broader context of program planning, behavioral objectives relate to the changes in behavior that the participants are expected to make that will address the health issues of concern.[4(pp141–143)] In this context, they relate to more long-term outcome behaviors of the participants.

1. Included but not limited to behaviors such as adherence, compliance, preventative action, and utilization of services.[4(pp143)]

2. Examples of behavioral objectives incorporating these concepts into an asthma program:

Six months following the asthma education program, 90% of participants will report that they:

- Participate in physical activities at least 5 hours per week. (adherence)

- Monitor their peak flow every morning and evening. (compliance)

- Take preventative medication prior to physical activities. (preventative action)

- Visit healthcare provider as needed based on self-monitoring of symptoms. (utilization of services)

Note: Each objective begins with a behavior or outcome (take, monitor, participate, visit); includes who will change (the participants); when or conditions (6 months after the program); how many or the criterion (90%).

F. Impact objectives (related to short-term impacts). This is a term that is used to encompass several types of objectives. It's what we are trying to change in the participants related to knowledge, skills, attitudes, and behaviors. Impact objectives include learning objectives, behavioral objectives, and environmental objectives.[2(p20),4(p143)] They relate to all of the aspects of how the participants will change because of the unit of instruction or program.[2(p20)]

1. May see evidence of impact during the program process or at the end of the program (short-term impact) or in the follow-up when long-term outcomes or impacts are evaluated.

- Example of an impact objective that would be assessed *during* the program or at the *end* and shows evidence of success: Participants attending the program will cut down on their smoking.

- In the long-term follow-up, the ultimate impact of the program is referred to as the *outcome* or *program objectives* as described next.

G. Program/outcome objectives. Relate to the final goal of the program.[4(pp143–144),6(pp62–64)] May be written as standards, such as in the model presented in this workbook. They usually cannot be measured at the end of the program, but rather they are determined in a long-term follow-up.

1. In a smoking cessation program, the ultimate program objective is for participants to stop smoking. They may do so at the end of the program (impact), but the long-term outcome may not be determined until later. Example:

In a 6-month follow-up survey, participants who stopped smoking by the end of the program will report that they have not smoked since.

2. May relate to morbidity, mortality, or quality of life. For example, in an asthma program, the following objective relates to morbidity and quality of life.

Participants in the asthma education program will have 50% fewer school days missed because of their asthma over the next academic year.

H. Environmental objectives. These are nonbehavioral objectives but create the atmosphere that helps participants achieve the ultimate goal of the program.[4(p143),6(p63)]

1. Relate to making changes in the environment that have an impact on the health issue of concern.[6(p63)]

2. May relate to the physical, social, or psychological environment.[4(p143)]

3. Examples from an asthma educational program:
   - During the first session, participants will be given protective mattress covers for their beds. (changing the physical environment to help control asthma symptoms)
   - By the end of the program, children will be allowed to carry their inhaler in school. (changing the social environment so that students will have immediate access to medication)
   - By the end of the program, children with asthma will have an after school support group available to them. (supporting the children by enhancing their psychological environment)

Part 2—Learning Objectives

This part of the chapter will address writing learning objectives for instruction in the 3 domains of learning. Like all objectives, they are developed from goals (program goals or goals for the specific unit of instruction).

A. Learning objectives are written in 3 domains as appropriate for the educational experience (lesson, unit of instruction, course or program).

1. **Cognitive:** concerned with intellectual skills, the learner's knowledge, and understanding (developed by Bloom and Krathwohl).[7]

2. **Affective:** concerned with the learner's values, attitudes, emotions, and ways of adjusting to illness (developed by Krathwohl et al).[8]

3. **Psychomotor:** concerned about skills requiring neuromuscular coordination, the actual performing of a skill (a version developed by Harrow[9] and then Simpson[10]).

B. The process for writing learning objectives is:

1. State the behavior or action related to what the learner will be able to do after the instruction.

Example from clinical practice: The patient will *perform* an inspiratory capacity using the incentive spirometer.

2. State the conditions placed on the learner.

Example: add to the aforementioned objective—*without assistance.*

3. State the standards of performance or how well the learner must perform. Refers to how often, how many times, how accurate.

Example: add to the aforementioned objective—*6 times per hour at 80% of preoperative inspiratory capacity.*

4. The complete objective is thus:
   - The patient will perform an inspiratory capacity using the incentive spirometer without assistance, 6 times per hour at 80% of preoperative inspiratory capacity.

5. Example of complete objective from health education: Given the labels of 10 foods (conditions), the children will choose (behavior) the 5 healthiest foods with 100% accuracy (standards).

Note: Sometimes it is not practical to include the conditions and standards in the objectives because they would be too wordy or not necessary. However, if they are not written into the objectives, they are stated and understood as part of the evaluation. This is especially important for participants when they are learning clinical skills or being evaluated for professional competence.

C. The format for writing learning objectives follows the style in the discussion on general objectives and specific learning outcomes. Example in the cognitive domain is presented here:

    1.0 The participants will understand the importance of prudent heart living.

        1.1 List the risk factors for coronary heart disease.

        1.2 Formulate a heart-healthy nutritional plan.

        1.3 Describe the effects that exercise has on maintaining a healthy lifestyle.

Common Errors in Writing and Using Objectives

A. Ignoring an essential domain. Example:

1. Writing the objective in the cognitive domain when the important part is for the learner to *perform* (psychomotor domain).

2. Underestimating the need to challenge the values and belief systems of the learner (affective domain) in order to accomplish a goal.

B. Writing objectives at the lower levels only. Example:

1. Emphasizing memorization of facts and including how participants will apply those facts.

2. Objectives that only *prepare* students for learning but do not address the final outcome.

C. Emphasizing what will be *taught* instead of what the learner is expected to be able to do. Example:

1. Emphasis on the *instructor*: To teach all of the levels in cognitive, affective, and psychomotor domains.

2. Emphasis on the *learner*: To write objectives at all levels in the cognitive, psychomotor, and affective domains.

D. Writing objectives related to the process vs. the outcome or the product. Example:

1. Process objectives will help the participant get there but is not stated in a measurable way. Examples:

    • The learner will *become more proficient* at writing objectives.

    • The learner will *gain more knowledge* in writing objectives in all 3 domains.

2. Product or outcome objectives indicate what the learner will be able to do in the end. Examples:

    • The student *will be able to write* objectives based on the criteria outlined in class.

    • The student *will be able to critique* objectives written in all 3 domains.

E. Using 2 verbs (behaviors or outcomes) in one objective. Examples:

1. *Create* and *evaluate* an instructional unit.

2. *List* the steps for writing objectives and *critique* objectives given on a quiz.

What Comes Next After Writing the Objectives?

A. Course content is developed based on the objectives.

B. Strategies are developed to assure the objectives can be achieved.

Part 3—Classification of Behavioral Objectives

These domains of learning were developed by Bloom and Krathwohl,[7] Krathwohl and colleagues,[8] Harrow,[9] and Simpson[10] beginning in the 1950s and have been widely used as a practical guide in all areas of education. In health education and health professional education, all 3 domains are important for planners to consider when writing objectives. In some units of instruction it will be important to write in all 3 domains, while in others only 1 or 2 are important.

Although Marzano and Kendall have developed a new taxonomy,[11] the original systems are presented here because they are well known to educators, they are still referred to in the literature, and they continue to work well as a guide for health education and program planning. In this overview, a sampling of verbs has been used for each level. A more comprehensive list of verbs can be found in Bloom and Krathsohl,[7] Krathwohl and colleagues,[8] Harrow,[9] Simpson,[10] and Marzano and Kendall.[11]

Cognitive Domain

Description and Examples of Verbs for Each Level[7]

1. Knowledge	Recalling or recognizing facts and ideas; remembering previously learned material; just requires bringing to mind the information.
	Examples: to list, define, name, underline, record, write, identify, locate, label, find, choose, state, select, repeat, recite, indicate, group.
2. Comprehension	Beyond just remembering information. The ability to grasp the meaning of information; understanding the message by translating from one form to another; or interpreting information; predicting the consequences or effects of things.
	Examples: describe, explain in different words, identify, restate, report, discuss, locate, draw conclusions, predict, outline, differentiate, rewrite, translate, estimate.
3. Application	Being able to use material or information in a new way; using principles, ideas, concepts or theories to problem solving.
	Examples: interpret, solve, utilize, illustrate, demonstrate, calculate, apply, classify, derive, modify, restructure, put together, relate, and transfer.
4. Analysis	A higher level of learning, because it requires knowing the concepts and how the material is organized. Breaking down information into its component parts so that it is understood how the parts are organized and relate to each other.
	Examples: analyze, appraise, diagram, differentiate, classify, categorize, examine, formulate, order, draw conclusions, make inferences, distinguish, debate, discover, form generalizations, explain.
5. Synthesis	Stresses creative behavior. Putting together parts to form a new whole; a new structure or plan.
	Examples: construct, create, write, formulate, organize, prescribe, design, develop, integrate, produce, modify, synthesize, revise, compose, generate.
6. Evaluation	Making judgments about material in terms of meeting criteria, which may be previously developed or designed by the learner. Requires achievement of all previous levels.
	Examples: assess, evaluate, judge, rate, rank, revise, score, appraise, measure, determine, optimize, select, conclude.

Examples of Objectives Written in the Cognitive Domain
Level   *Topic: Electrocardiography (EKG)*

1. Knowledge   Given a normal EKG, the student will label the P,Q,R,S,T waves.

                     Comment: This can be accomplished by recall, memorizing the facts.

2. Comprehension   Explain the electrophysiology of the heart as it relates to the normal EKG.

                     Comment: This requires a higher level of learning compared to the previous objective; the student must first be able to identify the PQRST waveforms, understand electrophysiology, and then relate it to what is happening on the EKG.

3. Application   Given a problem in the conduction system, predict the change that will occur on the EKG tracing.

                     Comment: This calls for using/applying knowledge of the principles of electrophysiology to determine what EKG change will result.

4. Analysis   Given an abnormal EKG, identify the arrhythmia.

                     Comment: This requires that the student has accomplished the previous objectives and is now putting that information together to analyze the situation.

5. Synthesis   Design a treatment plan for a patient who develops a specific arrhythmia.

                     Comment: This requires that the student has achieved the previous objectives. One must first identify that a problem exists and analyze what the problem is before creating a plan to solve the problem.

6. Evaluation   Evaluate the treatment plan for patients who have EKG abnormalities.

                     Comment: This is the highest level, and it assumes that the student has achieved objectives at all the previous levels. Before evaluating, it is necessary to be able to analyze related problems, consider how parts of the situation are organized and relate to each other, and be able to synthesize or create a plan of action.

Affective Domain

Description and Examples of Verbs for Each Level[8]

1. Receiving   Willing to direct attention to; becoming aware of; willing to attend to a particular matter.

                     Examples: receive, realize, reply, recognize, accept, attend.

2. Responding   Being willing to respond to; complying with an idea or suggestion; behaving in a suggested way; actively attending.

                     Examples: comply, react, observe, respond, cooperate, behave, examine.

3. Valuing   Accepting a value or behavior as a belief; preferring and pursuing that behavior, value, or belief.

                     Examples: accept, believe, prefer, influence, pursue, seek, value, defend, devote.

4. Organizing   Organizing a value or belief system into a structured relationship.

                     Examples: organize, relate, arrange, order, favor.

5. Characterizing an internally consistent value system   Integrating values and belief system into a philosophy of life. Acting with consistency regarding that value and belief system. Displays behavior accordingly.

                     Examples: internalize, verify, display, influence, practice (such as in lifestyle behavior).

Examples of Objectives Written for Each Level

Level	Topic: Developing an Exercise Program
1. Receiving	The participants will attend an information session addressing how to start an exercise program.

Comment: The lowest level only requires that the people attend the session and nothing more. |
| 2. Responding | The participants will discuss types of exercises that are most appealing.

Comment: The people are starting to get involved by showing some interest in discussing possibilities. |
| 3. Valuing | The participants will devote time and energy each day to an exercise program.

Comment: The people are showing that they are starting to adopt a value for exercise and are putting some importance on it. |
| 4. Organizing | The participants will organize their day to include an exercise plan at least 5 days per week.

Comment: The participants who achieve at this level have bought into the value of exercise and are organizing their lives around this preferred value. |
| 5. Characterization | The participants will have a standard of living that includes an exercise program.

Comment: Only the participants can really evaluate this level. Succeeding at this level requires that a person internalize a value system. Another person can only see evidence of this through behaviors but will not know if the behavior system is totally internalized just through observation. |

Psychomotor Domain

Description and Verbs Used for Each Level[10]

Level	Description
1. Perception	Being aware of objects or cues through the senses; relating those cues to motor acts.

Examples: hear, see, smell, taste, touch, distinguish, differentiates. |
| 2. Set | Being emotionally or physically ready to respond or to begin.

Examples: adjust, position, prepare, approach, respond, locate. |
| 3. Guided response | Repeating the performance of another person; practicing and gaining skills through trial and error. (This is the practice phase; guidance is needed.)

Examples: imitate, discover, repeat, copy, duplicate, build, manipulate. |
| 4. Mechanism | Responding to a situation or performing a task with a degree of self-assurance and skill. (This occurs as one is working toward mastery and is building up confidence.)

Examples: demonstrate, illustrate, indicate, manipulate, operate, adjust, set up, build. |
| 5. Complex overt response | Performing with certainty, with confidence, and with coordinated muscle control. (One is more confident; mastery is occurring with some tasks.)

Examples: demonstrate, maintain, operate, calibrate, coordinate. |
| 6. Adaptation | Varying basic motor acts to the meet the needs of new situations. (One is confident enough to make adjustments in performance.)

Examples: adapt, change, build, develop, adjust, alter. |

7. Origination	Develop new motor acts or ways of manipulating procedures or materials.
	Examples: construct, create, design, produce, develop, originate.

Examples of Objectives Written for Each Level

| Level | Topic: Operating Fitness Equipment
(Could apply to equipment in a variety of healthcare situations) |
|---|---|
| 1. Perception | The participant will become aware of various types of equipment in the fitness center. |
| | Comment: This could be accomplished with some orientation where the participants just observe their surroundings. |
| 2. Set | The participants will adjust the equipment to the assigned settings. |
| | Comment: This is showing a readiness to proceed or getting; set to go; for example, adjusting the Nautilus equipment to the suggested settings. |
| 3. Guided response | The participants will imitate the instructor's demonstration of the exercises using the equipment. |
| | Comment: This is the demonstration/return demonstration strategy; guidance from the instructor is needed; in complicated procedures this practice phase will take more time than for less complicated procedures. |
| 4. Mechanism | The participants demonstrate their ability to utilize the equipment with minimal help from the instructor. |
| | Comment: Confidence is being built with some proficiency; this will take more or less time depending on the degree of difficulty. |
| 5. Complex overt response | The participant will operate the equipment without hesitation and without assistance. |
| | Comment: Confidence is building and the participant is working toward mastery. |
| 6. Adaptation | The participant is able to change the settings on the equipment as strength is developed. |
| | Comment: Participant is able to adapt as more confidence and skill are developed. |
| 7. Origination | The participants will create an exercise program using the equipment to meet their needs. |
| | Comment: This can occur when they are confident enough in the motor acts that they can manipulate the procedures to meet new demands/needs. |

Constraints Related to Writing and Using Objectives

1. There may not be sufficient time for all the learners to achieve at the competency level.
2. Sometimes the academic system or the healthcare system restricts the amount of time one can spend with learners.
3. Not everyone learns in the same way. Some participants may need alternative strategies to achieve the objectives.
4. The instructor may incorrectly assume that the students have the prerequisite knowledge for the objectives.
5. Success may, in part, relate to the attitudes and values of the participants, and the instructor may not have sufficient means of addressing this.

Helpful Hints for Writing and Using Objectives

1. Address the constraints to limit them as much as possible.

2. Not all levels or all domains need to be included in a specific program or unit of instruction. Write objectives only in the domains and levels that apply.

3. When objectives are all written at the higher levels, it is assumed that the lower levels are already achieved or will be covered in the program.

4. One class may deal with lower level objectives with further development related to the higher level objectives in subsequent classes.

5. When participants do not perform a psychomotor skill, consider if they are missing cognitive knowledge about the skill.

6. Some difficult skills may not be mastered for a long time. For example, in learning to drive a car, real mastery doesn't occur until sometime after one earns a license. At first, a lot of conscious thought goes into every move when driving a car, until one day the driver realizes that he got somewhere without thinking about every maneuver.

7. During the practice phases of learning complicated tasks, people often appear to be doing a lot of work and complain of being very tired. This happens to clinical students who may question their choice of a profession. It is helpful to point out that this is normal, and that as confidence and skill are developed, they will not be so tired.

Questions
Part 1—Cognitive Objectives

1. Consider the project you are developing. Write at least 1 objective for each level in the cognitive domain that relates to your topic. Remember that this is for practice. Each level may not be appropriate for your specific project.

   Knowledge

   Comprehension

   Application

   Analysis

   Synthesis

   Evaluation

2. Do a self-assessment of your objectives by going through this checklist.

   _____ Have you used an *action* verb that can be measured?

   _____ Have you used only *one* verb for each objective?

   _____ Are the *conditions* specified where appropriate?

   _____ Are the *standards* specified where appropriate?

   _____ If you used a general objective first, do you have specific objectives that clarify the general objective?

   _____ Are your objectives written for the learner and not related to what the instructor will be doing?

   _____ Are all your objectives product oriented and not process oriented?

   If you answered "no" to any of these questions, review related information in this chapter and then rewrite the objectives as needed.

Part 2—Affective Objectives

1. Write objectives for each level in the affective domain. Remember that this is for practice. Each level may not be appropriate for your specific project.

   Receiving

   Responding

   Valuing

   Organizing

   Characterizing an internally consistent value system

2. Do a self-assessment of your objectives by going through this checklist.

   _____ Have you used an *action* verb that can be measured?

   _____ Have you used only *one* verb for each objective?

   _____ Are the *conditions* specified where appropriate?

   _____ Are the *standards* specified where appropriate?

   _____ If you used a general objective first, do you have specific objectives that clarify the general objective?

   _____ Are your objectives written for the learner and not related to what the instructor will be doing?

   _____ Are all your objectives product oriented and not process oriented?

   If you answered "no" to any of these questions, review related information in this chapter and then rewrite the objectives as needed.

Part 3—Psychomotor Objectives

1. Consider a topic that includes the psychomotor domain. (The project you intend to do for class may or may not include this domain. If it does, use your project topic.) Write at least 1 objective for each level in the psychomotor domain.

   Perception

   Set

   Guided response

   Mechanism

   Complex overt response

   Adaptation

   Origination

2. Do a self-assessment of your objectives by going through this checklist.

   _____ Have you used an *action* verb that can be measured?

   _____ Have you used only *one* verb for each objective?

   _____ Are the *conditions* specified where appropriate?

   _____ Are the *standards* specified where appropriate?

   _____ If you used a general objective first, do you have specific objectives that clarify the general objective?

_____ Are your objectives written for the learner and not related to what the instructor will be doing?

_____ Are all your objectives product oriented and not process oriented?

If you answered "no" to any of these questions, review related information in this chapter and then rewrite the objectives as needed.

3. Write down any questions you have about writing objectives in general or related specifically to your unit of instruction or the program you are developing.

Practice Cases

Here are the 3 cases you worked on in previous chapters. Write objectives that fit the case to include the many types of objectives you learned to write in this chapter. Compare with your classmates and work together to assure you have covered all the possible types of objectives that could apply to the situation. Check that they work toward reaching the program goals you wrote previously.

Case 1: Healthcare Clinic

You are an employee in a healthcare clinic. Your supervisor has asked you to create a program to decrease the risk of H1N1 flu in current employees and patients who visit the clinic.

Case 2: After School Program

You volunteer at an after school program for children in grades 3 through 5. Currently, they complete their homework, participate in craft projects, and have a snack. You think it might be a good idea to add physical activity and nutrition components to the existing program. Your supervisor agrees and asks you to develop a proposal for this.

Case 3: Pharmacy

You are an intern at a local pharmacy. Many clients come in to ask questions of the pharmacists about preventing the onset of certain diseases. You realize it would be a good idea to have a series of wellness lectures about obesity, diabetes, cardiovascular disease, and hypertension. Your supervisor says that this will be a great program for you to develop.

References

1. Timmreck TC. _Planning, Program Development, and Evaluation, A Handbook for Health Promotion, Aging, and Health Services._ Sudbury, MA: Jones and Bartlett; 2005.
2. Gilbert GG, Sawyer RG. _Health Education—Creating Strategies for School and Community Health._ 2nd ed. Sudbury, MA: Jones and Bartlett; 2000.
3. Hayden J, ed. _The Health Education Specialist: A Study Guide for Professional Competence._ 4th ed. Whitchall, PA: The National Commission for Health Educational Credentialing, Inc; 2000.
4. McKenzie JF, Neiger BL, Thackeray R. _Planning, Implementing, and Evaluating Health Promotion Programs._ San Francisco, CA: Pearson Education, Inc; 2009.
5. Gronlund NE, Brookhart SM. _Writing Instructional Objectives._ 8th ed. Columbus, OH: Prentice Hall; 2009.
6. Hodges BC. _Assessment and Planning in Health Programs._ Sudbury, MA: Jones and Bartlett; 2005.
7. Bloom BS, Krathwohl DR. _Taxonomy of Educational Objectives. Handbook I: Cognitive Domain._ New York, NY: Longman; 1984.
8. Krathwohl DR, Bloom BS, Masia BB. _Taxonomy of Educational Objectives, Handbook II: Affective Domain._ New York, NY: McKay; 1964.
9. Harrow AJ. _A Taxonomy of the Psychomotor Domain: A Guide for Developing Behavioral Objectives._ New York, NY: Longman; 1972.
10. Simpson EJ. _The Classification of Educational Objectives in the Psychomotor Domain._ Washington, DC: Gryphon House; 1972.
11. Marzano RJ, Kendall JS. _The New Taxonomy of Educational Objectives._ 2nd ed. Thousand Oaks, CA: Corwin Press; 2007.

CHAPTER
6
Teaching Strategies

Chapter Objectives

- Describe types of learning styles.
- Analyze your own learning style.
- Design learning strategies that meet the needs of different learning styles.
- Describe considerations specific to patient education.
- Identify criteria for providing psychological support to patients.
- Utilize effective presentation skills.
- Summarize the process for using each learning strategy in the chapter.
- Describe strategies to reduce constraints that may interfere with the learning system process.

Introduction

The purpose of this chapter is to give students a variety of practical strategies to use when teaching individuals and groups. The first consideration in choosing strategies is to realize that not everyone learns in the same way. Teachers tend to use strategies that they experienced themselves and what worked for them as students. This chapter will explain a variety of strategies that focus on meeting different learning styles.

Learning Style Description

A. Learning style is the way an individual prefers to understand, interpret, organize, process and think about information.[1(pp273–277),2(pp3–4)]

1. Refers to the ways in which people take in facts and ideas, store, and later remember the information.[2(pp3–4)]

2. Not everyone learns in the same way, and it's important for participants to understand that one learning style is not better than another.

3. Individuals have dominant learning styles, although over time, people adapt to many styles.

B. Why it is important to understand learning styles:
   1. Helps explain the differences observed in how participants learn.
   2. Justifies developing a range of teaching strategies to build on different strengths of individuals.
   3. Important to consider our own learning style and how it impacts our teaching style.

Activity: Ask participants to take one of the many learning style inventories available in both print and on the Internet. Have them analyze the results and describe how it matches what they have experienced.

Using Learning Styles to Develop Teaching Strategies

A. Consider that individuals have different learning styles, and developing different strategies will help meet varying needs.[1(pp273–277),2(pp1–14)]

   Learning styles are categorized into 3 types:[2–5]
   1. Visual learning—includes reading and writing
   2. Auditory learning—includes listening and speaking
   3. Kinesthetic learning—includes visualizing and manipulating

B. Visual learners learn through reading and writing. They learn if they can see information, picture something in mind, read directions instead of hear them, or rewrite directions in their own words.[2(p5–9),5]
   1. Visual learners do better when illustrations are used while the instructor is speaking. They like to take notes while listening.
   2. Examples: PowerPoint slides, video clips, charts, diagrams, handouts, tours of environment where learning or patient care will take place.
   3. Participants might want to close their eyes and picture what is being said.
   4. Have written materials available for participants to read.
   5. Participants may benefit from reading the material prior to a class or presentation.
   6. Participants may enjoy keeping a journal or a log of activities, writing reports, or writing a story about what they are learning.

C. Auditory learners learn through listening and speaking. They process and learn information more easily by listening and discussing.[2(pp5–9),4,5]
   1. Auditory learners like lectures and discussions; they may like to work in groups to talk with others.
   2. They may *not* want to take notes, but will process the information through listening and then talking about it.
   3. Participants may want to record the presentation or discussion and listen again.
   4. Suggest to patients that they record information about their health issue as it is provided to them.

D. Kinesthetic learners learn through visualizing and manipulation. They learn through hands-on strategies, taking things apart and putting things together.[2(pp5–9),4,5]
   1. Participants may like lab situations, demonstrations and practice, building things, making posters, and organizing portfolios of their work.
   2. Encourage participants to handle materials and equipment or build models.

Connecting Learning Styles to How People Remember

A. Many authors have referenced an adaptation of Edgar Dale's *Cone of Experience*[6] to suggest how people generally remember.[7(p45),8(p71),9]

B. Although the percentages may not be exact, it's the relativity that is important to think about when designing learning strategies.

C. People generally remember[7(p45),8(p71),9]:

    1. 10% of what they read

    2. 20% of what they hear

    3. 30% of what they see

    4. 50% of what they hear and see

    5. 70% of what they say or discuss

    6. 90% of what they do or say

Teaching Considerations for Effective Learning

A. Learning will be more effective if a participant sees a need for it.

B. Feedback is important during the learning process.

C. Learning must be reinforced.

D. Learning is retained when information is put to immediate use.

E. Connect learning to real life experiences whenever possible.

F. Plan alternative strategies for participants who do not achieve objectives through primary strategies.

G. Keep participants involved!

Teaching Patients

Considerations for teaching in a clinical environment or other setting when working with patients include the following[10(pp48–55)]:

A. Use language they will understand.

B. Choose an appropriate time; don't compete with something else.

C. Control the environment—privacy, comfort, and sufficient time.

D. Consider patient/learner readiness to process information, including attention to:

    1. Pain control and stability.

    2. Family member involvement as needed.

    3. Any barriers to processing information.

    4. Impaired senses.

E. Fear of discussion or unfamiliar surroundings may impact ability to take in information.

F. Keep patients involved in the learning process!

G. Provide psychological support.

    1. Acknowledge feelings and behaviors.

    2. Develop a trusting relationship by being honest and nonjudgmental and by listening.

    3. Build on the positives:

        • Acknowledge even small accomplishments.

        • Look for signs of strength and help individuals build upon them.

Lecture Format for Presentations

A. Why lectures are used frequently:

    1. Efficient way to give a lot of information in a short amount of time.

    2. Can summarize information from a variety of sources.

3. Give up-to-date information.

4. Can be used for any size group.

B. Problems with lectures:

1. Do not always encourage active participation on the part of the learner.

2. May not promote critical thinking unless additional strategies are used.

3. Information may be lost unless strategies are used for reinforcement.

C. Three components to the lecture process:

1. The introduction:

- Introduce the topic.
- Discuss why it is important and how they will use the information.
- Refer to goals and objectives of the presentation.
- Relate the topic to material previously presented.

2. The presentation:

- Develop major points with examples.
- Use additional strategies for critical thinking.
- Insert cases or situations that show relevance of the information.
- Use visual aids such as PowerPoint slides.

3. Summary of the important points:

- Review how the information will be used.
- Use strategies and assignments for reinforcement.
- Help participants self-assess what they learned.

D. Strategies to improve the lecture method:

1. Get participants involved by beginning with a case study or case example that brings meaning to the topic and relates to their experience.

2. Have participants work in groups for a short time:

- Brainstorm what they know about the topic before beginning.
- Work on case studies to help them process the information.

3. Ask open-ended questions during the lecture.

- Allow time for everyone to think before calling on someone to answer.
- Have students come up with answers in pairs or small groups and then report and discuss with the entire group.
- Be conscious of who participates and use strategies to help everyone be involved.

4. Give examples and tell stories during the presentation.

5. Be attentive to and respond to nonverbal feedback from participants.

6. Inform the group about how the information relates to subsequent presentations.

7. End the class by getting anonymous feedback from the participants (See the discussion on one-minute paper in the "Sample Types of Formative Evaluation Methods" section in Chapter 8).

Case Studies

A. Can be incorporated with other strategies or used to reinforce information.

B. A way to help participants apply new knowledge to problem-solving situations and connect to what they already know.

C. Can teach objectives at the higher levels, such as application, analysis, synthesis, and evaluation.

D. An effective way to teach about ethical situations, how to problem solve or to consider different points of view on issues.

E. Summary of a suggested case study process:

   1. Present the case in writing with questions for participants to consider.

   2. Have them work by themselves first and then in pairs or small groups.

   3. Ask participants to consider how their responses differ from others.

   4. Reunite as a large group and share what they regard as the best responses.

   5. Have a discussion about important issues that arise.

   6. Summarize major points and relate to the general topic being presented.

Case Study Example: Ethical Dilemma

You are involved with a continuing education program for professionals who need the hours for licensure renewal. They are required to attend the entire day and then have their form signed to indicate attendance. A participant who is your friend asks if you will sign his form after lunch because he is being called back to work.

1. Describe your initial reaction to the situation.

2. How would you respond? Justify your response then take the opposite viewpoint.

3. Is there any other information that could change your perspective on this situation?

4. What are the ethical issues involved in this situation?

5. More ideas for creating and using case studies can be found in Davis,[1(p222–228)] Gilbert and Sawyer,[8(p115–116)] and *Study Guides and Strategies*.[11]

Role Playing

A. Role playing will appeal to auditory and kinesthetic learners.[5]

B. Role playing is done to act out real life problems or situations.

C. Possible uses are to teach communication, conflict resolution,[12] responsibility,[13] and problem solving.[14]

D. Role playing is used to prepare for situations and to practice how to handle them.

E. Role playing can be done to practice and develop skills important in helping situations.

F. A summary of a format for role playing follows[15,16]:

   1. Define and write out the objectives.

   2. Describe the situation and set the context.

   3. Describe who is involved and what their roles are to be.

   4. Introduce the role-play and set the ground rules.

   5. Ask participants to volunteer to take a part.

   6. May allow observers to try alternative questions when the players get stuck.

   7. Process the role-play with the players and then the audience.

   8. Review the situation and discuss what happened during the role-play.

   9. Ask the audience if they have any alternative suggestions for what could have occurred.

   10. Debrief and discuss with the group what they learned and how to transfer what happened to other situations.

   11. More ideas for creating and using role-plays can be found in Davis[1(pp229–232)] and Gilbert and Sawyer.[8(pp156–158)]

Role-Play Example

Participants are in a group designed to help them advocate for themselves about healthcare needs.

Objective—Develop skills to advocate needs with landlords about healthy living conditions.

Situation—You recently moved into an urban city apartment building. Since moving to the new location, you have had symptoms that your physician indicates are allergic type symptoms. Tests come back indicating you are allergic to mold. You determine that there is mold in the apartment and you need to approach the landlord. Other people have told you that he is difficult to deal with and slow to react. You are looking for some ideas of how to approach him. You are thinking about moving out but you would lose a deposit that you cannot afford.

Players—The landlord and the person with the health problem.

Journal Writing and Activity Log

A. These are strategies that will appeal to visual learners and those who enjoy writing.[2,5]

B. Strategies to help participants keep track of behaviors and activities.

C. To make visible the small steps of progress made toward a goal.

D. To heighten awareness of thoughts and emotions surrounding a behavior.

E. To become more aware of circumstances surrounding an event or behavior.

F. Helps participants to make plans based on new insights recognized through their journals or logs.

Writing Example 1

In keeping an exercise log, the participant became aware that she stayed with her program when she had a specific destination for her daily walk. This resulted in her making a new plan to walk to the coffee shop each morning. The result was an increase in motivation and miles per week.

Writing Example 2

In keeping a dietary journal, a participant realized she had been underestimating her caloric intake. In reviewing her journal the leader helped her to recognize the errors in estimating the amount of food she was eating. With some new strategies she was able to get back on track and ultimately meet her weight goals.

Brainstorming Session

A. Will appeal to participants who like to express themselves by talking and discussing.

B. To gather a lot of ideas about a problem or issue in a short amount of time.

C. Can be a strategy used to gather needs assessment information.

D. Can serve as a group effort toward problem solving.

E. Summary of brainstorming format. For other pointers on brainstorming see Gilbert and Sawyer,[8(pp113–115)] Brainstorming Process,[17] Dominguez,[18] and Glazer.[19]

   1. Introduction:

      • Describe the topic or problem and why it is significant.

      • Relate to the brainstorming session objectives.

      • Assure participants that their responses will not be judged.

      • May assign a recorder; tape the session or write responses on paper or on a board.

      • Should not in any way be intimidating for the participants.

      • Set a time limit for the session.

2. The session:

- Have participants volunteer their ideas.

- Encourage everyone to participate.

- Continue until there are no more ideas or the time limit is up.

- Facilitator may help by giving hints at the end if ideas slow down.

3. Summarize the ideas:

- Describe how ideas may be used.

- Connect to other related topics.

- The group may vote on solutions or come to consensus depending on the issue at hand.

- Keep in mind that the purpose may be to determine a variety of ways to look at a situation and not to come to a solution.

Example of Brainstorming Questions

1. What strategies can be implemented to improve our connection with the community in developing health education programs?

2. What are some steps we can take to reduce the stress level for patients while they are in the hospital?

3. What are some of the professional attributes important for health educators to exhibit?

4. What are some strategies that the department could initiate for more efficient use of staff time and still provide quality programs?

Site Visits or Tours

A. A strategy used to introduce participants to a new environment. For example:

1. Open house at a community center where new wellness education programs are planned.

2. Tour of clinical facility where students will be doing their practical experience.

3. Tour of a facility to prepare a person for being admitted.

B. Helps participants who are visual learners and need to picture the environment to feel comfortable.

C. May be done virtually using technology.

D. May combine with observation as a needs assessment strategy. For example:

1. Visit to a school to observe choices students make in the cafeteria.

2. To observe types of physical activities students engage in during recess.

3. To experience an environment to help with career decision making.

E. Depends on the situation. Some guidelines:

1. Make any arrangements with the facilities involved with the visit.

2. Write out the objectives and communicate to participants.

3. May give questions to participants to help focus their attention.

4. Encourage note taking.

5. Where necessary, review proper conduct at healthcare facilities.

6. In patient care situations, the visit may include family members.

7. Following the visit, help participants process their experience.

8. Answer questions and summarize important points.

9. Review objectives to be sure they were accomplished.

Games

A. Games involve strategies to make learning fun.

B. Games can be played in groups or by individuals.

C. The types of games are only limited by the imagination of the leader.

D. The format and process are developed based on the type of game being played.

E. Objectives and the process are developed by the leader.

F. Rules are put in writing and are explained verbally to the participants.

G. When the game is ended, the leader facilitates a discussion about what was learned.

H. The goals and objectives of the game are reinforced.

Examples of Games That Could Be Developed

Most games are used to review information.

1. A Jeopardy game for competing individuals or teams (Jeopardy templates can be found online).

2. Two teams playing a college quiz bowl type of game—teams of participants work together to come up with answers faster than the opposing team.

3. A scavenger hunt to find things and places as part of an orientation.

4. Matching labels on things that need to be learned.

5. Crossword puzzles for terminology (templates are available online).

6. Explore virtual possibilities and keep up with technology advances.[1(p231)]

7. Create your own game designs! For other ideas for using games see Davis,[1(pp229–232)] and Gilbert and Sawyer.[8(pp168–171)]

Demonstration Method

A. This method is used to show how to perform a task or a procedure.

B. Consider the stages of developing psychomotor skills in Chapter 5.

C. The instructor demonstrates and then the participants imitate demonstration.

    1. The instructor may need to do a task analysis first.

    2. The instructor should break down procedure into parts.

    3. Participants first practice and demonstrate parts of the procedure or task.

    4. As they develop competence, they demonstrate the entire procedure.

D. This strategy works toward developing the psychomotor skills. For example:

    1. The correct way to use exercise equipment.

    2. Learning procedures involving clinical skills.

    3. Practicing skills for independent living or to take care of self.

E. This strategy will appeal to the kinesthetic learners, those who like to manipulate things, and to visual learners who benefit from seeing a situation.[2(pp5–9),4,5]

F. Those who don't have this learning style as a strength may need more time to practice and build confidence. Ways to help them include:

    1. Use guidance as they practice.

    2. Talk through the procedure as they perform.

    3. Give feedback as they go through the performance.

G. The demonstration process follows:
   1. Write objectives of the demonstration and share with participants.
   2. Incorporate strategies for other learning styles:
      - Use written materials of the procedure (*readers*)
      - Show procedure on video (*visual learners*)
      - Talk through the procedure (*auditory learners*)
      - Encourage participants to take notes (*writers*)
   3. Watch for common errors and demonstrate again, emphasizing the correction of the errors.
   4. Reinforce skills by encouraging participants to help each other as they gain competence.
H. In evaluating participants on a procedure, assess if performance problems are related to the:
   1. *Cognitive domain*—Learners need knowledge to be reinforced.
   2. *Psychomotor domain*—Learners have difficulty in neuromuscular coordination in performing the skill.
   3. *Affective domain*—Does the participant appreciate the need to learn the skill?

Discussion Method

A. Communication between participants and facilitator.
B. Purpose is to review material or make connections between material and real life situations.
C. Can take on many different formats, but the following apply to preparing for most discussions:
   1. Write out the objectives and communicate them to participants.
   2. In preparation, give participants background information through lecture; readings; observation; real life experience.
   3. Decide on the format (small groups, class as a whole, etc.).
   4. Write down the main points to be discussed.
D. The discussion:
   1. Let students address each other as much as possible.
   2. Assure that everyone is respectful of each other's opinions and views.
   3. Make statements or answer questions where appropriate.
   4. Observe student participation level and try to get everyone involved by directing some questions to specific individuals.
   5. Point out connections (or help students make connections) when possible.
   6. Formulate transitions between topics at the appropriate times.
   7. Make summary statements.
   8. List all possibilities for decisions or conclusions.
   9. Lead students to make the best decision, if appropriate.
   10. Review goals and objectives to assure they have been addressed.
   11. For more information about using the discussion method, see Davis,[1(pp97–105)] *Beyond the Talk*,[20] and *The Human Rights Education Handbook*.[21]

Materials for Teaching

A. Materials for teaching are tools used for individual instruction or to enhance learning when used in combination with other strategies.
B. Materials help participants with different learning styles.
C. Written materials should be at the appropriate reading level for the audience.

D. PowerPoint (PPT) slides are commonly used for presentations.

   1. The following are selected criteria for developing PPT slides[22]:

      • For title—Use 32-pt font at a minimum.

      • Text in bullets—Set text at a 20-pt minimum.

      • Rule of 6—Limit text to 6 lines per slide and 6 words per line.

      • Outline—Slides should be an outline of the presentation.

      • Colors—Choose colors that have a contrast and will be visible.

   2. Practice your presentation in the room where presenting, if possible.

      • Check how slides show in the room.

      • Make adjustments as needed in font size; color scheme.

      • Determine the best place to stand during the presentation.

   3. For more pointers for PowerPoint presentations, see Davis[1(pp453–457)] and Clark.[22]

E. Models help participants learn through seeing and handling objects. These can be actual models for students to handle or computer models.

   1. Models can help students who learn through manipulation and visualization.

   2. Write objectives for the purpose of the models and communicate with participants.

   3. Give some guidance as to how the models should be used.

Examples of Models

1. Model of the heart and vessels for teaching about heart disease.

2. A model of the food pyramid for teaching nutrition.

3. Model of the respiratory system for teaching participants about asthma.

4. Numerous virtual models for teaching dissection as well as many other concepts.

F. Computer-assisted instruction is used as a primary learning strategy or to supplement other strategies or for remediation; it is most often used for individual instruction.

   1. Write objectives as to the purpose of the computer-assisted instructions and communicate those to the students.

   2. Many new computer programs have been developed over the past several years to enhance learning and build problem-solving skills.

   3. Be sure to preview programs prior to assigning them to the participants.

   4. Use only part of the computer-learning tool if that is all that is applicable to the objectives.

   5. Assure that participants have instruction on using the computer tool.

   6. For more ideas about using computer assisted instruction, see Gilbert and Sawyer.[8(pp116–118)]

Group Learning

A. Group learning is used to help students process and reinforce information and skills.

B. Group learning is used to help develop the skills to work as part of a team.

C. Participants may be assigned to a group for one session or for an extended period of time (for example, the entire semester).

D. Being part of a team reinforces the participants' strengths and builds confidence.

E. Group learning gives students an opportunity to reinforce learning through peer teaching.

F. When using group work, keep the following in mind:
1. The purpose and the objectives should be communicated to the group.
2. The leader should help participants set the ground rules.
3. The leader helps to create a comfortable environment for group interaction and a positive experience.

G. Helpful hints for group work, brainstormed with senior level health science students based on their experience, are as follows:
1. Be sure the assignments among participants are equal.
2. Have participants write action plans for completing their work.
3. Make the assignment so the work can be divided into tasks among the participants.
4. Participants want formative feedback on their group projects.
5. Ground rules should include: show respect, be punctual, be supportive of each other, be open to constructive criticism, be willing to give feedback, be flexible, and be willing to vary the leadership.

Constraints Related to Teaching Strategies

A. Strategies can simulate but not replace some environments.
B. Participants may have cognitive/psychomotor limitations.
C. The instructor may need to use group strategies when individual instruction could be more effective.
D. More time and alternative strategies may be needed to achieve the expected level of competency.

Questions

1. Take one of the learning styles inventories available online. How do the results match up to what you believe is/are your dominant learning style(s)? Describe an experience you have had in learning that illustrates your style. Remember that there is not one best type!

2. Describe all of the strategies you would like to use to teach your unit of instruction. (Remember that the strategies presented in this chapter are only samples; other ideas may come from your experience.)

3. Describe what learning styles are met by using each strategy. In what way have you incorporated the concepts of how people remember?

4. Look back at your objectives. Identify how each objective will be met by the teaching strategies.

5. Anticipate constraints that may occur given each teaching strategy and discuss ways to limit or prevent each problem.

6. Describe any barriers to effective teaching and communication that apply to your program and your participant population. What steps will you take to overcome the barriers?

7. What will you do to provide psychological support and a positive environment for the participants? (This will vary depending on the type of program or learning unit.)

8. Do a self-evaluation of your strategies by going through this checklist:

_____ Have you written strategies for every objective?

_____ Do the strategies address all the different learning styles?

_____ Have you written strategies for reinforcement and to help participants process the information?

_____ Do you have alternative strategies for the participants who do not accomplish the objectives?

_____ Do you have a plan for limiting any barriers that affect teaching and communication?

_____ Do you have a plan for providing support and for creating a positive environment for the participants?

If you answered "no" to any of these questions, consider again how you can address the problems identified.

9. Write down any questions you have about teaching strategies in general or specifically to your unit of instruction.

Practice Cases

Here are the 3 cases you worked on in the previous chapters. This time, design learning strategies for the objectives that you wrote. Be sure all are covered and that you meet the needs of participants with different learning styles. Compare with your classmates and work to come up with an array of possibilities.

Case 1: Health Care Clinic

You are an employee in a healthcare clinic. Your supervisor has asked you to create a program to decrease the risk of H1N1 flu in current employees and patients who visit the clinic.

Case 2: After School Program

You volunteer at an after school program for children in grades 3 through 5. Currently, they complete their homework, participate in craft projects, and have a snack. You think it might be a good idea to add physical activity and a nutrition component to the existing program. Your supervisor agrees and asks you to develop a proposal for this.

Case 3: Pharmacy

You are an intern at a local pharmacy. Many clients come in to ask questions of the pharmacists about preventing the onset of certain diseases. You realize it would be a good idea to have a series of wellness lectures about obesity, diabetes, cardiovascular disease, and hypertension. Your supervisor says that this will be a great program for you to develop.

References

1. Davis BG. _Tools for Teaching._ San Francisco, CA: Jossey-Bass; 2009.
2. Sonbuchner GM. _The Learning Styles Handbook for Teachers and Tutors._ Bloomington, IN: Author House; 2008.
3. Shirley R. _Which One Are You? World Wide Learn._ http://www.worldwidelearn.com/education-articles/how-do-you-learn.htm. Accessed March 15, 2010.
4. Chrislett M, Chaptman A. _Free VAK Learning Styles Test._ [Businessballs free online learning]. http://www.businessballs.com/vaklearningstylestest.htm. Accessed March 15, 2010.
5. Barsch J. _Barsch Inventory._ http://ww2.nscc.edu/gerth_d/AAA0000000/barsch_inventory.htm. Accessed March 15, 2010.
6. Dale E. _Audio-Visual Methods in Teaching._ 3rd ed. Holt, Rinehart and Winston; 1969.
7. Hayden J, ed. _The Health Education Specialist: A Study Guide for Professional Competence._ 4th ed. Whitehall, PA: The National Commission for Health Educational Credentialing, Inc; 2000.
8. Gilbert GG, Sawyer RG. _Health Education—Creating Strategies for School & Community Health._ 2nd ed. Sudbury, MA: Jones and Bartlett; 2000.
9. Anderson HM. _Successful Teaching Excellence Perspectives for Pharmacy Educators—Dale's Cone of Experience._ http://pharmacy.mc.uky.edu/faculty/resources/files/Step%20Dales%20Cone.pdf. Accessed March 15, 2010.

10. Watson ME. A systems approach to patient education. In: Litwack K, ed. *A Core Curriculum for Post Anesthesia Nursing*. 4th ed. Philadelphia, PA: WB Saunders; 1999.
11. *Study Guides and Strategies—Case Studies*. www.studygs.net/casestudy.htm. Accessed March 15, 2010.
12. Wadsworth J. Conflict Resolver to Conflict Creator: Thoughts on Writing Mediation Roleplays. *Conflict Manager in Higher Education Report*. 2003. http://www.campus-adr.org/CMHER/ReportArticles/Edition3_3/Wadsworth3_3a.html. Accessed March 15, 2010.
13. Lyde A, Temple M. Health Education in Practice. Let's Party: Teaching Responsible Alcohol Consumption Through Role Play. ERIC EJ572713. http://www.eric.ed.gov/ERICWebPortal/custom/portlets/recordDetails/detailmini.jsp?_nfpb=true&_&ERICExtSearch_SearchValue_0=EJ572713&ERICExtSearch_SearchType_0=no&accno=EJ572713. Accessed March 15, 2010.
14. *Why Use Role-Playing. Starting Point—Teaching Entry Level Geoscience*. http://serc.carleton.edu/introgeo/roleplaying/reasons.html. Accessed March 15, 2010.
15. *How to Teach Using Role-Playing. Starting Point—Teaching Entry Level Geoscience*. http://serc.carleton.edu/introgeo/roleplaying/howto.html. Accessed March 15, 2010.
16. *Role-Playing Games and Activities Rules and Tips*. http://www.businessballs.com/roleplayinggames.htm. Accessed March 15, 2010.
17. *Brainstorming Process—Brainstorming Technique for Problem-Solving, Team Building, and Creative Process*. 2009. http://businessballs.com/brainstorming.htm. Accessed March 15, 2010.
18. Dominguez P. *IDEO's 7 Rules for Brainstorming*. 2008. http://www.greenbusinessinnovators.com/7-rules-of-brainstorming-from-ideo. Accessed March 15, 2010.
19. Glazer P. *Brainstorming 101—How to Stretch Your Team's Capacity for Innovation*. January 25, 2007. Teambuildinginc.com—A division of Team Builders Plus. http://www.teambuildinginc.com/article_brainstorming_101.htm. Accessed March 15, 2010.
20. *Beyond the Talk. San Francisco Unified School District. Discussion Method*. 2009. http://www.beyondthetalk.org/resources/facilitation/discussion-method. Accessed March 15, 2010.
21. *The Human Rights Education Handbook. Effective Practices for Learning, Action and Change. Method 6: Discussion*. http://www1.umn.edu/humanrts/edumat/hreduseries/hrhandbook/methods/6.htm. Accessed March 15, 2010.
22. Clark N. *Guidelines for Professional Presentations for Student Presentations-Effective Professional Presentation Skills*. 2006. http://www.authorstream.com/Presentation/Mudki-27950-Effective-Professional-Presentation-Skills-Objectives-Body-Language-Clearly-Audience-Involveme-as-Entertainment-ppt-powerpoint. Accessed March 15, 2010.

CHAPTER
7

Interventions and Behavior Change Models

Chapter Objectives

- Explain the behavior change models illustrated in this chapter.
- Describe strategies of intervention for each construct of the behavior change models.
- Incorporate a behavior change model into your program project.
- Describe how to use health communication theory to help change behavior.

Introduction

In the previous chapter, a variety of teaching strategies were suggested to assist participants in learning information to help them achieve program goals and objectives. The strategies take into consideration that people have different learning styles and that a variety of teaching strategies are used to help people learn or move toward adopting a healthy lifestyle. However, people do not change their behavior just based on knowledge. If that were true, all people would exercise and eat healthy foods, and no one would smoke. The purpose of this chapter is to introduce behavior change models and intervention strategies to help participant populations move forward with achieving personal behavior change to ultimately work toward their goals.

Choice Theory will be explained as a general planning process to help individuals make behavior changes. This theory is included because is it based on self-evaluation and is helpful for working with individuals or with participants in a group setting.

Then three additional types of behavior change theories will be described: an intrapersonal theory (the Health Belief Model), an interpersonal theory (Social Cognitive Theory), and a community level theory (Health Communication Theory).

Choice Theory

Choice Theory was developed by William Glasser.[1,2] This theory is based on internal control psychology that is used in counseling, education, and management as a way to help people gain more effective control of their lives. It is based on the belief that all individuals have 4 basic psychological needs in addition to survival and physiological needs. These needs are thought to be genetic, and it is thought that each of us is constantly trying to satisfy them. Having an understanding of Choice

Theory can help individuals work toward making behavior changes. The major concepts as described by Dr. Glasser are summarized here[1,2]:

A. All behavior is internally motivated (as opposed to external control).

B. Since we each *choose* our behaviors, we can learn to make better choices.

C. Behavior is total and has 4 components: thinking, acting, feeling, and physiology. The 2 components that we have the most control over are thinking and acting. When we think differently about a situation and take an action, feelings and physiology move in a different direction.

D. Our behavior is our best attempt to satisfy our basic needs. These include physiological needs to survive as individuals and as a species and these 4 psychological needs:

   1. *Belonging*—love, cooperation, a sense of connection with others.

   2. *Power*—gaining importance, a sense of achievement, feeling accomplished.

   3. *Fun*—having pleasure in life, a sense of enjoyment.

   4. *Freedom*—having independence and autonomy, and the ability to make choices and express oneself freely.

E. To use this theory in helping participants to make behavioral changes, assist them in self-evaluating what they really want. Ask them:

   1. What goal do you want to achieve?

   2. What is the underlying reason for this goal?

   3. What behavior change(s) will help you work toward your goal?

   4. How will you be different or how will it make your life better by making this behavior change?

   5. Is making this behavior change worth the time and effort?

F. Help participants prepare for the behavior change by asking: What preparation is necessary to carry out your plan? For example:

   1. If planning to exercise, what clothes are needed; when will you exercise, and what routine do you have to change to include exercise?

   2. In making a plan to eat healthier, what exactly do you need to purchase, or what is needed to change your routine in order to bring food to work or school?

G. Help the participants plan for potential barriers to their plan by asking:

   1. What barriers may prevent you from carrying out your plan?

   2. How can you prevent or limit these barriers?

   3. How can you carry out your plan when problems arise? For example:

     • What can you plan to do if the weather doesn't allow you to exercise outdoors? An alternative plan may be to walk at an enclosed mall.

     • What will you do if time does not allow you to put together a healthy lunch before going out the door? An alternative might be to have something prepared ahead of time in the freezer to take out on busy mornings.

H. Help participants identify how they will evaluate the plan by asking:

   1. How will you record progress?

   2. What will success look like to you?

   3. How will you know when you are successful? This should reflect back on the underlying purpose of the plan. For example:

     • In the case of exercise, the participant may feel better or have better muscle tone.

     • In the case of healthier eating, success may include loss of weight, decrease in cholesterol levels, or feeling more confident.

I. Help participants with timelines by asking them:

    1. When will you begin?

    2. By what date will you complete the plan?

J. Help participants self-evaluate their level of commitment. Ask them:

    1. How committed are you to carry out this plan?

    Note: Participants are not likely to carry out a plan if they are not committed. Be sure the plan belongs to the participant and not the helper.

    2. If you are not fully committed, what plan could you commit to that will help move you toward your goals?

K. Help participants to evaluate their success. Ask them:

    1. How successful were you in carrying out your plan? For example, how many days did you exercise or take your lunch to work?

    2. What did you accomplish of which you were the most proud? For example, being able to complete an exercise plan on your busiest day.

    3. If you were not completely successful, what specifically could you have done differently?

    4. Are you interested in working on a new plan or adjusting your plan?

    5. If participants are interested in starting a new plan or making adjustments, help them work through the planning process again. The second time developing a plan usually is accomplished more quickly.

L. Keep a positive emphasis throughout the process. Help participants to emphasize what they *did* accomplish and not what they *did not* accomplish. For example, when the plan was to exercise 3 times, and they only exercised once, instead of asking about the *nonexercise* days, ask about what the *circumstances* were that resulted in the 1 day of exercise. The idea is to do more of what worked instead of concentrating on what did not work.

Activity: Choose a behavior change or goal that you would like to make. Use the questions to go through the process of planning for your own behavior change. The purpose of this activity is to gain appreciation for how difficult it can be for program participants to make behavior changes. Remember that baby steps are more achievable than giant steps when you first begin to make a change.

Health Belief Model

The Health Belief Model (HBM) was first developed by psychologists in the Pubic Health Service in the 1950s to explain why so few people were taking advantage of free screening programs such as those for tuberculosis.[3,4(pp45–62)] The HBM has continued to be developed over time and is a commonly used theory in health education. The HBM predicts health behaviors based on the beliefs and attitudes that people have toward health issues and diseases.[4(p46),5(pp31–35)]

A. The decision to take action on a health recommendation is based on the beliefs and perceptions about the health issue.

B. Individuals weigh their beliefs and perceptions against each other in making a decision to act. In this model, changing perceptions is the key to encouraging people to act on heath information and advice. A short description of the HBM constructs is given here. A more extensive description can be found in Champion and Celette[4] and Hayden.[5]

    1. *Perceived susceptibility*—the fear a person has about getting a disease or the risk felt toward a condition. The tendency to act depends on how susceptible a person feels about the problem.[4(p47),5(p31)]

       • *For example:* A woman who has been exercising regularly and has engaged in healthy behaviors for 25 years may not feel susceptible to having a heart attack. She may ignore signals of a heart attack because of the belief that it is not possible with her healthy history and the belief that women are not as likely as men to have heart attacks.

- *Strategies to help:* Increase knowledge and awareness; educate about the risks if not seeking medical attention when confronted with the symptoms; give examples of women athletes who have had heart attacks; give information about the susceptibility and that women are most likely to ignore symptoms.

2. *Perceived seriousness*—the belief about how significant the problem would be if one did get the disease or condition. The tendency to act depends on personal perception of the how severe the problem will be.[4(p47),5(p31)]

- *For example:* The previously discussed health-conscious woman may believe that even when a heart attack does occur, it will not be serious because of excellent overall health.

- *Strategies to help:* Educate about the cost and consequences of the problem; use case studies of women athletes who have suffered a heart attack to illustrate potential severity of the problem.

Note: Perceived susceptibility and perceived seriousness work together to develop a sense of perceived threat a person feels toward the health problem.[4(p42)] The more a person fears the problem or situation, the more likely he or she is to take action.

3. *Perceived benefits*—refers to the perception of how one will benefit from taking the action. What strategies and resources are available to prevent the health problem, and how much will that action help?[4(p47),5(p32)]

- *Strategies to help:* In our continuing situation, teach the woman about appropriate actions that can be taken when heart symptoms occur and the positive outcomes expected from taking the action. What does she believe will really help in limiting the consequences if a heart attack does occur? Help to change the existing perceptions of the benefits of taking early action. Discuss the cost with her if no action is taken (for example: in terms of recovery, time, money, and emotional energy).

4. *Perceived barriers*—the obstacles that will prevent taking action to adopt the health behavior.[5(p33)] Individuals weigh possible benefits with potential barriers.[4(p47)]

- *For example:* The following may occur: The woman ignores symptoms because of the perception that it couldn't really be a heart attack. The barrier is that she is very busy and doesn't have time to spend in the emergency room to find out that it's just pain from a workout injury. The *belief* is that taking action will be such a waste of time. *Perception* is that maybe a couple of aspirin will be enough.

Note: The woman weighs the inconvenience of spending time in the emergency room (barriers) and the perceived benefits of getting early treatment for the heart attack. The person who feels an overall sense of good health may make a decision that it is not worth the time.

- *Strategies to help:* Provide information on the effects of not seeking treatment (in terms of morbidity and mortality, cost to self and family). Encourage self-evaluation of the financial and emotional cost/benefit of allowing whatever barriers would prevent seeking treatment.

Note: Perceived benefits and barriers work together and are weighed or judged along with the level of threat a person feels as a decision is made to take action or not.

5. *Cues to action*—triggers (events, people, or things) that encourage a person to engage in a behavior.[5(p33)] These are strategies that increase awareness of the problem or remind people about taking an action.

- Ask the individual what cues to action will serve as an incentive. For example: carrying a picture or having a picture in the office of what motivates her to live; having a postcard on the refrigerator as a reminder of signs and symptoms of heart attack and steps to take when having symptoms; having aspirin available to take when faced with symptoms of a heart attack; and learning CPR to help others encountering a heart attack may serve as a reminder to take action for herself as well.

6. *Self-efficacy*—the confidence a person feels in his or her ability to take action.[5(pp34-35)]

    • *For example:* The person makes a decision that the amount of time spent to receive medical attention is possible for him or her and is worth it.

    • *Strategies to help:* Provide information on how to take the action of seeking medical attention. In the action steps, include where to go and any precautionary treatment to take prior to making it to the emergency room.

Activity: The following case is designed to help you process how to incorporate the HBM into health education programs.

The European Union wants to set volume limits on MP3 players to help limit hearing loss. Action is necessary because there is concern over health risks, especially to younger people. A European Union scientific body estimates that up to 10 million Europeans could suffer health loss from listening to MP3 players at unsafe volumes. High volumes sustained over time can lead to permanent hearing loss.[6]

A. Is it necessary to implement government standards for MP3 players because young people are not taking action to prevent hearing loss?

B. Brainstorm with your group what the thinking might be for each construct of the HBM.

C. What would be some interventions for each construct to help people change their behavior?

Social Cognitive Theory

Social Cognitive Theory (SCT) was developed by Albert Bandura. This theory is based on reciprocal determinism and the interaction between personal factors (such as knowledge, attitudes, and psychomotor abilities along with experience), the environment, and behavior.[5(p81),7-9(pp167-180)] The theory indicates that the 3 factors are connected and work together. When one factor is changed, all factors are affected.[5(p81)]

A. SCT is an example of an interpersonal theory of health behavior. People are influenced by their social environment, and the environment is influenced by the individuals.

B. The environment is anything that is external to the individual, including the social environment (for example, family, friends, colleagues, classmates) and the physical environment (for example, a new physical fitness center, the availability of food, a classroom setup, and temperature).[9(p168)]

C. Consider this situation as an example as the major constructs are explained: People in a given community are thinking about working out but have no convenient place that is cost effective. Then a university builds a workout center and invites people in the community to use the facilities free of charge for 2 hours per day.

D. A summary of the major SCT constructs is presented here. A more extensive description can be found within these references.[5(pp81-85),9(pp167-185)]

    Note that some of the constructs have been described together for this example because the strategies to help are similar.

    1. *Behavior capability and self-efficacy*—Does the person have the knowledge and skills to perform the activity or behavior? Does he or she have enough confidence in his or her abilities?[5(p84),9(p171)]

        • *For example:* People in the community need to know that they have the skills to use the center.

        • *Strategies to help:* Invite the people into the center and give them training on the equipment. Set up group fitness activities and offer personal training sessions to build skills and confidence.

2. *Expectations and expectancies*—What are the potential results of engaging in the behavior, and do people value the potential outcomes?[5(p84),9(p171)]

   - *For example:* What outcomes can people expect from regular exercise, and will they value those results?

   - *Strategies to help:* Explain the potential effects of exercise and help participants with realistic expectations. Help participants self-evaluate what they really want and whether the hard work is worth it to them.

3. *Locus of control and reinforcements*—These are factors that increase the likelihood that a participant will continue with the behavior. How does one perceive the control over a situation? Does the participant have internal control or is the person controlled by external forces?[5(p84)]

   - *For example:* Are the participants motivated because the fitness center is free (external control) or are they motivated to work out because of the benefits to their health? Do either of these factors need reinforcement?

   - *Strategies to help:* Have friendly weight loss contests or a competition for the number of hours people work out in a given time period. Competition can be an incentive to motivate participants, especially while building up the routine of regular exercise. Personal training and group sessions with feedback can serve as reinforcements.

4. *Observational learning*—This refers to knowledge and skills gained by watching or studying what others do. It is learning through role modeling and peer learning.[5(p81),9(p171)]

   - *For example:* Fitness participants can learn through group fitness sessions and by watching others work out.

   - Strategies to help: Assure that the trainers have the skills to do the personal training and group sessions so that participants have the proper role modeling.

5. *Self-control*—Participants gain control over behavior through self-monitoring and altering behavior.[9(p171)]

   - *For example*—Participants are gaining control over their behavior of working out.

   - *Strategies to help:* Encourage participants to keep a journal or a log of their workout activities. Monitor the circumstances when they *did* work out. The idea is to help them adjust their circumstances to do more of what worked when they did go to the fitness center.

6. *Emotional arousal and coping response*—This construct is for people to learn and engage in a behavior they need to be able to deal with the anxiety surrounding the situation.[10(p187)]

   - *For example:* Going to an unfamiliar place such as a fitness center can cause a feeling of anxiety, especially if the person is obese.

   - *Strategies to help:* Assist participants to feel comfortable by giving tours of the fitness center. Engage them in group sessions and personal training to build skills and confidence. Give positive reinforcement.

Activity: The following case is designed to help you process how to incorporate Social Cognitive Theory into your health education program.

High school students learned in health class that a high-fat diet can lead to obesity and other health problems. The cafeteria does not offer low-fat alternatives. As a result, they have requested to go out for lunch. However, it is against school policy to leave the building during school hours. The administration is willing to work with the students to help with solutions.

A. What are the issues that surround this problem, and what are the solutions?

B. Who should be involved with the discussion?

C. Brainstorm with your group the thinking for each construct of Social Cognitive Theory.

D. Describe strategies for each construct of SCT to help solve the problems.

Health Communication Intervention Strategies (HCIS)

The National Cancer Institute and the Centers for Disease Control and Prevention define health communication as strategies designed to inform and influence individual and community decisions about health.[11] Almost all health education programs include health communication as part of their intervention.[10(p203)]

A. Communication strategies include a variety of ways to get the message out to the priority population with the goal of influencing health behavior. The following suggestions for making decisions about communication strategies are summarized from the National Cancer Institute[11]:

   1. Identify the health problem and consider if communication should be included in the intervention.

   2. Consider the audience and decide the best way to reach them.

   3. Pilot test the communication messages and materials with the target audience.

   4. Use pilot results to make changes and then implement the health communication program.

   5. Evaluate effectiveness and modify as needed.

B. Specific health communication strategies include the following channels[10(pp203–206)]:

   1. *Intrapersonal*—one-on-one communication (such as communication between an individual and the healthcare provider).

   2. *Interpersonal*—communication with groups (such as a health education seminar or group presentation and discussion).

   3. *Mass media*—broadcasting (such as radio and television), Internet media (such as blogs, message boards, podcast, and video sharing) and in print messages (such as newspapers, magazines, journals, posters, postcards, and flyers).

   4. *Organization and community strategies*—reaching people and getting the health message out through organizations in the community (such as churches, organization newsletters, or other places where people are actively involved and will see or hear the message).

Activity: Consider the case described earlier about the European Union, which wants to set volume limits on MP3 players to preserve hearing. Action is necessary because there is concern over health risks, especially to younger people.

   1. Identify the health problem and consider if communication should be included in the intervention.

   2. Who is the target population and what communication strategies will reach them?

   3. What messages and materials would you develop?

   4. How would you evaluate the effectiveness of the messages and materials?

Questions

After reading this chapter on interventions and behavior change models, respond to the following questions:

   1. Consider a project you would like to develop. Describe your target population.

   2. What behavioral change model(s) will be best for your population?

   3. Describe what your population may be thinking for each construct of the model(s) you choose.

   4. Describe the behavior change strategies you will incorporate into your project to help participants move forward with their goals.

   5. What health communication messages are needed for your program and what channels of communication will you use?

   6. Write down any questions you have about interventions and behavior change models.

Practice Cases

Here are the 3 cases you worked on in the previous chapters. This time, consider health behavior change models and communication strategies to work with the target populations.

Case 1: Healthcare Clinic

You are an employee in a healthcare clinic. Your supervisor has asked you to create a program to decrease the risk of H1N1 flu in current employees and patients who visit the clinic.

1. Describe the target population.

2. Explain what the participants might be thinking in terms of the HBM constructs. What interventions would you suggest in working with them?

3. Explain what the participants might be thinking in terms of the SCT constructs. What interventions would you suggest in working with them?

4. What health communication messages are needed? Suggest the methods of communication you would use.

Case 2: After School Program

You volunteer at an after school program for children in grades 3 through 5. Currently, they complete their homework, participate in craft projects, and have a snack. You think it might be a good idea to add physical activity and nutrition components to the existing program. Your supervisor agrees and asks you to develop a proposal for this.

1. Describe the target population.

2. Explain what the participants might be thinking in terms of the HBM constructs. What interventions would you suggest in working with them?

3. Explain what the participants might be thinking in terms of the SCT constructs. What interventions would you suggest in working with them?

4. What health communication messages are needed? Suggest the methods of communication you would use.

Case 3: Pharmacy

You are an intern at a local pharmacy. Many clients come in to ask questions of the pharmacists about preventing the onset of certain diseases. You realize it would be a good idea to have a series of wellness lectures about obesity, diabetes, cardiovascular disease, and hypertension. Your supervisor says that this will be a great program for you to develop.

1. Describe the target population.

2. Explain what the participants might be thinking in terms of the HBM constructs. What interventions would you suggest in working with the participants, given the constructs?

3. Explain what the participants might be thinking in terms of the SCT constructs. What interventions would you suggest in working with the participants, given the constructs?

4. What health communication messages are needed? Suggest the methods of communication you would use.

References

1. Glasser W. *Choice Theory: A New Psychology of Personal Freedom*. New York, NY: HarperCollins; 1998.
2. Glasser W. *Choice Theory: The Ten Axioms of Choice Theory*. http://www.choicetheory.com. Accessed December 10, 2009.

3. Hochbaum GM. *Public Participation in Medical Screening Programs: A Sociological Study.* Washington, DC: Government Printing Office; 1958 PHS publication no. 527.

4. Champion VL, Celette SS. The health belief model. In: Glanz K, Rimer BK, Viswanath K, eds. *Health Behavior and Health Education.* 4th ed. San Francisco, CA: Jossey-Bass; 2008.

5. Hayden J. *Introduction to Health Behavior.* Sudbury, MA: Jones and Bartlett; 2009.

6. *Consumers: EU Acts to Limit Health Risks from Exposure to Noise from Personal Music Players.* http://europa.eu/rapid/pressReleasesAction.do?reference=IP/09/1364. Accessed December 10, 2009.

7. Bandura A. *Social Cognitive Theory.* Englewood Cliffs, NJ: Prentice Hall; 1977.

8. *Personality Theories: Albert Bandura.* http://webspace.ship.edu/cgboer/bandura.html. Accessed March 23, 2010.

9. McAlister AL, Perry CL, Parcel GS. Social cognitive theory. In: Glanz K, Rimer BK, Viswanath K, eds. *Health Behavior and Health Education.* 4th ed. San Francisco, CA: Jossey-Bass; 2008.

10. McKenzie JF, Neiger BL, Thackeray R. *Planning, Implementing, and Evaluating Health Promotion Programs.* San Francisco, CA: Pearson Education; 2009.

11. National Prevention Information Network. http://www.cdcnpin.org/scripts/campaign/strategy.asp. Accessed December 12, 2009.

CHAPTER

8

Evaluation

Chapter Objectives

- Given a specific learning unit or program, describe the purposes of evaluation.
- Differentiate between:
  - a) Product and process evaluation.
  - b) Norm-referenced and criterion-referenced evaluations.
  - c) Formative and summative evaluations.
- Develop formative evaluation methods to use throughout the learning process.
- Develop summative evaluation instruments.
- Describe how to use formative and summative evaluations to improve the learning system.
- Critique your evaluations using criteria for each type of instrument.
- Consider principles of validity and reliability when writing and using evaluation instruments.

Introduction

The purpose of this chapter is to provide basic evaluation concepts and strategies for students learning to teach and learning to develop program planning skills. Ideas for considering the purposes of evaluation will be described. Definitions associated with evaluation will be presented along with examples of how and when they would be used. Information will be given about actually writing and using different types of evaluation instruments. Sample evaluations can be found in Appendix B.

Determine the Purpose of Evaluation

A. Evaluation to make decisions before and during the process of the program for the purpose of improving the effectiveness (process evaluation—part of formative assessment).[1(p188),2(p144),3(pp337-339),4(p50)]

  1. How is the program going?

  2. Are there any administrative tasks that were overlooked?

3. Do any logistics need to be adjusted such as schedule or environmental concerns?

4. What else is needed to put the program in the best position to be successful?

B. Evaluation for the purpose of feedback during the program (formative assessment).

1. To help the participants in the process of learning.

2. To help the instructor decide what changes need to be made in strategies or materials so objectives will be achieved.

C. Evaluation to make decisions at the end of the program or course.

1. What grade should be given (in cases where it is required)?

2. Are the students ready for professional practice?

3. Should the program continue to be offered? Is it worth the cost?

4. To gather information about how the program can be improved.

D. Evaluation to determine if the goals of the program were successful (summative evaluation).

1. Have essential competencies been achieved?

2. Have goals, standards, and objectives been met?

3. How has the program changed the behavior, knowledge, or skills of the participants?

4. Consider what is necessary and possible to measure in terms of short- and long-term evaluation.

E. Evaluation to contribute to the scientific literature or to inform policy decisions.[3(p340)]

1. What data will contribute to future programming?

2. What data may impact policy decisions and shape the larger community?

Determine What Types of Evaluations Are Needed

A. Formative evaluation (process evaluation) is done during the program planning process and during the program itself. The purpose is to check that the program is running as intended and to improve the program. Assessment of learning throughout the program is done to assure that instruction is effective and to make adjustments so that participants have the best possible opportunity to achieve the objectives.[1(p188),2(p144),3(pp337–339),4(p50)]

1. Formative assessment prior to the start of the program (which may include pilot testing) answers the following questions for planners or instructors about whether they are set to begin:

   • Are all the tasks done to implement the program?

   • Are all the materials together?

   • Are the resources (funding, personnel, physical) set for the program?

   • Have all contacts been made?

   • What other support is needed?

2. Formative assessment during the program from the perspective of the participants answers questions such as:

   • How is the program going for them?

   • Are they learning useful information and skills?

   • Is the environment conducive to learning?

   • What else do they need to succeed?

3. Use information to make adjustments in strategies and anything else needed to help participants achieve the program objectives.

B. Summative evaluation determines if the program was successful. It includes both impact and outcome evaluation, and it answers the questions:

1. Did the program do what it intended to do?

2. Were the goals and objectives and outcomes of the program achieved?

3. Was there a cause and effect between the program and the outcome?[1(p188)]

4. Was the program successful?

5. Did the program deliver as it was expected to do?

6. Have the goals and standards and objectives of the program been met?

C. An impact evaluation determines what happened because of the program; it is used to evaluate changes in the short-term program goals and objectives.[2(p144)] Using this evaluation answers questions about whether the program influenced the participants. For example:

1. Did the participants start exercising during the program?

2. How many participants stopped smoking by the end of the program?

3. Did participants make an appointment with a dermatologist for a skin check-up as a result the program?

D. An outcome evaluation is done to assess the final results of the program; it is used to determine if long-term program goals were met; to evaluate the product of the program; to determine if quality of life improved; and to assess any improvement in morbidity, mortality, and health status.[1(pp188–190),2(pp144–148),3(p339)] Examples:

1. Did the quality of life improve for the families of children with asthma?

2. Did the number of reported cases of early onset diabetes increase with the city-wide education program?

3. Did the pass rates go up with the implementation of the review program?

4. Has the program had a long-term impact on participants?

   - If a participant permanently changed behavior because of the program it would be a long-term outcome (example: exercising regularly over time, yearly visits to the dermatologist).

   - Participants who live a healthier lifestyle and improve their health status over time illustrate a long-term impact.

   - In health professional education, a long-term outcome would be the graduates' becoming licensed and practicing their profession.

Developing and Implementing Formative Methods of Evaluation

A. Review administrative tasks to assure everything is in place for the program.

B. Ask questions to determine understanding during the process of instruction.

C. Observe and document participant behaviors.

D. Assess knowledge, skills, and attitudes.

E. Provide self-assessment materials to participants.

F. Ask participants to document how they have changed.

1. How new knowledge/skills have been used.

2. Attitudes about behaviors/situations encountered.

3. Problem areas that need attention.

4. Self-perceived abilities, skills, and attitudes.

G. Give the instructor concurrent feedback and indicate what is working or not working.

Sample Types of Formative Evaluation Methods

A. Objective written assessments such as quizzes and tests given throughout the process of instruction.

B. Oral questioning during the learning process.

C. Direct observation—rating scales and checklists. (See Appendix B)

D. Same instruments may also be used as self-evaluation for participants.

    1. How do the participants feel about their progress?

    2. What is going well for them and what is not going well?

    3. Is there anything they would like to change that would be helpful for their learning progress?

E. One-minute papers—a method for getting formative feedback from participants by asking them to respond in writing about the questions posed by the instructor at the end of class.[5(pp290–291),6]

    1. Ask participants to answer 2 questions about the presentation or class.

      • What was the key point (or major concepts) in class today?

      • What are you still confused about?

    2. Answering 2 questions will take about 1 minute for the students to write and 1 minute for the instructor to read.

    3. The instructor will get a sense of how successful the presentation or instruction was.

    4. It will become evident as to what questions the students have as a group.

    5. Often a pattern is seen as to the confusion over concepts.

    6. If done consistently, students will be focused during the presentations regarding what they are getting and what they are confused about.

    7. The instructor can begin the next class clearing up the questions from participants.

    8. Alternative questions for 1-minute papers:

      • How is this program going for you?

      • What changes would you like to see made?

      • In what way has this program changed your behavior?

      • What changes are you going to make as a result of what you learned today?

F. Physical assessment and laboratory data, for example:

    1. Has there been improvement in range of motion in an exercise program?

    2. Has there been improvement in blood sugar levels in a diabetic education program?

    3. Were cholesterol levels expected to decrease after an exercise program was initiated?

    4. Use information to make appropriate changes in the individual plan.

G. Continuous analyzing process.

    1. Consider information from 1-minute papers, quizzes, or tests.

    2. What objectives have been accomplished?

    3. What needs to be explained again?

    4. What knowledge or skills need to be reinforced?

    5. Implement alternative teaching strategies where needed.

H. Problems with domain(s) of learning.

    1. Cognitive domain—knowledge deficiency.

    2. Psychomotor domain—problem with the actual performance of a skill requiring neuromuscular coordination.

    3. Affective domain—problem with performance because attitudes or values have not been developed.

Developing and Implementing Summative Methods of Evaluation

A. A summative evaluation is an evaluation at the end of instruction to assess program impact or long-term outcome results.

B. Summative evaluations assess mastery of learning, the product, or outcome of learning. They may be used to determine readiness to progress. For example:

   1. To leave the unit of a healthcare facility.

   2. To live independently.

   3. To practice a profession.

C. Were goals, standards, and objectives achieved?

D. Long-term outcomes include changes in health status and changes in morbidity and mortality rates.

   1. It is not usually possible for a single program to show these results since they are long term.

   2. In a single program, one may only be able to see the immediate impact or short-term success.

E. You may use the same methods as in formative evaluations, for example:

   1. Checklists, rating scales.

   2. Objective-type tests.

   3. A combination of methods to assess cognitive, psychomotor, and affective domains of learning.

F. A summative evaluation for a professional program may include:

   1. Success on professional exams.

   2. Success in obtaining professional employment.

   3. Follow-up surveys of employers of graduates.

   4. Follow-up satisfaction survey of graduates after they have been practicing their profession.

   5. Percentage of participants completing the program over time.

G. A summative evaluation for a health education program may include:

   1. Assessment of participant satisfaction.

   2. Follow-up surveys to patients, families, or caregivers.

   3. Changes in behavior, knowledge, attitudes, or skills.

   4. Questions about what they are doing differently because of the program.

H. A summative evaluation in patient education may include:

   1. Statistics on specific complications.

   2. Morbidity and mortality rates.

   3. Number of emergency room visits.

   4. Number of repeat participants.

I. Use this information to adjust parts of the process where needed. For example:

   1. Were the program goals and standards achieved?

   2. New considerations in performing needs assessments.

   3. Modify or add to the objectives.

   4. Develop more effective strategies for teaching and reinforcement.

   5. Make adjustments in the program and reevaluate over time.

Process and Product Evaluation in Assessing Skills

A. During a process assessment, the instructor will be measuring the performance of a procedure.[7(p276)] For example:

   1. Can the participant perform the procedure correctly?

   2. Can the student perform the steps to do an X-ray properly?

   3. Can the participant perform the exercises using the correct form?

B. The product is the end result of the performance.

   1. Did the performance result in a quality X-ray?

   2. Did the performance result in accurate data?

   3. Did the exercise program prescribed bring about positive results?

Norm-Referenced and Criterion-Referenced Evaluations

A. Norm-referenced tests report performance relative to the other people.[7(pp39–42)]

   1. These results do not tell instructors what the individuals are able to do, only how they stand in relation to others.

   2. It is possible on such a test for a student to get a score of 40% and still pass the exam if the class did poorly as a whole.

   3. It is possible for a student to pass a course with a low average, never actually showing achievement of the material.

   4. In health professional education, norm-referenced testing is not acceptable because a practitioner must be competent to practice specific skills.

B. Criterion-referenced evaluations give information in terms of the behavior or performance a participant is able to demonstrate.[7(pp39–42)]

   1. The level of acceptable performance is known before instruction.

   2. Objectives are defined in behavioral (performance) terms.

   3. Standards of performance should be clearly specified.

   4. Such evaluations require that test items be selected on the basis of the specified behaviors delineated in the objectives.

   5. Criterion-referenced evaluations require a scoring system that reflects actual student performance related to the identified behaviors.

   6. The goal is for everyone to be successful if they can all pass the competencies.

   7. Health professional education requires that graduates be able to perform all the identified competencies, independent of the performance of others. For example:

      • It is not acceptable for students to pass 9 out of 10 identified skills (even though they demonstrated 90% of the skills).

      • If that 10th skill is essential for professional practice, then it doesn't matter how well the student did on the other skills, in terms of being clinically competent.

Developing and Using Valid Evaluations

A. Validity is the extent that a test or evaluation actually measures what it intends to measure.[3(p118),7(pp70–73)]

B. The validity of a test relates to what the test measures and how well it does so.[3(p118),7(pp70–75)] For example: A multiple-choice test would not be a valid way to determine how well a person can perform a skill.

C. Face validity addresses whether the evaluation appears to measure what it is supposed to measure.[7(p76)]

   1. Carefully look at the evaluation instrument.

   2. Does it appear to measure what it is intended to measure?

   3. This is not a trustworthy measure in itself, but it is a place to begin.

D. Content validity is the extent to which an evaluation measures the intended content of a course or program.[7(pp74–80)]

   1. Occurs during the test construction.

   2. Does the test contain a sampling of all major aspects of the content and in the desired proportion?

   3. Do the questions match the objectives?

   4. Do the number of test items related to specific content areas correlate to the amount of time spent on each area?

E. Criterion-related validity is the extent that an evaluation predicts an individual's performance in specified activities. Performance on the test is measured against a criterion.[7(pp85–95)] There are 2 types of criterion validity about which to be concerned:

   1. Predictive validity—the extent that a test or evaluation predicts what will happen at another time.[7(pp86–87)] The test scores are collected at one point and then measured against a criterion at a future time. Examples:

     • Does entrance criteria predict who will be successful in a program?

     • Does the practice exam predict who will be successful on the exam taken for licensure or certification?

     • Does successful performance of a skill in a clinic result in the ability to do the same at home?

   2. Concurrent validity—the criterion measured against the test scores validated at approximately the same time as the test or evaluation.[7(p86)] Relates to concurrent behaviors rather than future performance. Examples:

     • Choosing science as a self-perceived ability should correlate with good science grades.

     • A person scoring high on an eating disorders inventory should exhibit signs and symptoms of eating disorders.

     • A person describing signs of depression should show results of depression on an instrument to measure depression.

Developing and Using Reliable Tests and Evaluations

A. Reliability refers to the consistency of scores or ranking obtained by an individual over a period of time.[7(pp107–113)]

B. Are the test results reproducible? Reported as a correlation coefficient, reliability may be demonstrated in several ways:

   1. *Test-retest reliability*—repeating the identical test at a different time or day.[7(pp110–111)] (If the test has reliability, a participant should get approximately the same score each time.)

   2. *Alternate-form reliability*—using alternative forms of the same test.[7(p112)] (Scores should be independent of which form was used.)

   3. *Split-half reliability*—dividing the test in half and determining a score for each half.[7(pp112–114)] (This is a way to look at a test that has items written by 2 instructors.)

4. *Interrater reliability*—the ability of 2 people to use an evaluation instrument and have the same results.[7(pp115–118)]

- This is an essential point to consider in evaluating the performance of a student for clinical proficiency.
- This is important in any type of observation evaluation.
- The goal of interrater reliability is for the evaluation to be a true measure of the participant's ability independent of who did the evaluation.
- It is important for evaluators to be trained to use the instruments.

5. Reliability may be influenced by:

- Quality of evaluation/survey items.
- Number of items (too many or too few items).
- Physical and emotional state of participants.
- What directions are given to participants.
- Experience of the evaluator.
- Environmental factors, for example:
  - A. Room too cold or warm
  - B. Uncontrollable noise
- Rapport between the participant and the evaluator.

C. Practical ways to improve the reliability of tests/evaluations include:

1. Develop instruments and surveys that go through a critiquing process by expert professionals.
2. Assure that the directions are clear.
3. Develop a scoring system that is consistent, clear, and objective.
4. Indicate the critical incidents that delineate who passes and who does not.
5. Standardize the conditions as much as possible, for example:
   - What instructions will be given to participants?
   - How much time will be given for participants to perform a procedure?
6. Educate the evaluators on how to use the evaluation instruments.

Helpful Hints for Writing All Types of Questions

A. Key the questions to the objectives (content validity).
B. Have a colleague review the test (face validity).
C. Ask an equal number of questions related to each content area (unless one area is more important).
D. The goal is to write a fair test that distinguishes what a student knows and does not know.

Writing Multiple-Choice Test Items

A. One best response and 4 or 5 alternatives.
B. What to avoid:

1. Open-ended questions in which the student must look at the alternatives to know what is asked.
2. Questions in which the correct answer is uncertain.
3. Always and never (they are often wrong).

4. Trivial fact questions (instructors sometimes do this to make a question difficult, when the trivia may not be important).

5. Purposefully tricky questions (keep in mind that the goal is to test the knowledge and skills of participants and not their ability to guess what the instructor is thinking).

6. Extraneous information that serves only to confuse test taker.

C. Considerations:

1. Underline or capitalize significant words such as <u>NOT</u>.

2. All responses should be about the same length.

3. Distractors should be plausible.

4. Be sure to test at the level intended (check objectives).

5. Randomize the position of correct answers.

6. Allow about 1 minute for each question.

D. More information on writing multiple choice tests in Davis and Miller and colleagues.[5(pp390–400),7(pp194–217)]

Writing Case Study Types of Tests

A. Usually to test problem-solving ability.

B. Simulates a situation in which the participants are likely to be.

C. Begins with a short case scenario followed by multiple-choice items, short answers, or both.

D. Guidelines to consider:

1. Each question should stand alone and not depend on the answer to a previous question (unless this is the intention).

2. Avoid giving information in the responses that indicate the answer to another question.

What Analyses Are Practical to Do on Multiple-Choice Tests?

A. Measurements of central tendency—allow comparisons to be made from one group to another and for students to see how they did in comparison to the class.

1. *Mean*—the average score.

2. *Median*—the middle score.

3. *Mode*—the most frequent score.

B. Item analysis—a review of the frequency of responses for the purpose of checking items:

1. For ambiguity.

2. For poorly written items.

3. To determine if there could be an alternative correct answer.

4. To discover a mistake in documenting the correct answer on the score sheet.

C. Reviewing individual test items:

Example 1: (*correct answer)

	A	B	C	D
Frequency of responses	40*	0	0	0

Comment—This item may be too easy, but in a criterion-referenced test, this may be just an indication of success and the desired outcome of learning.

Example 2: (*correct answer)

	A	B	C	D
Frequency of responses	3	15*	20	2

Comment—Check answer C to determine if there was a mistake, or whether C is just a plausible distractor.

Example 3: (*correct answer)

	A	B	C	D
Frequency of responses	10	9	10*	11

Comment—Check this test item carefully. It is clear that students did not know the answer and perhaps got it correct by guessing.

Example 4: (*correct answer)

	A	B	C	D
Frequency of responses	2	3	7	28*

Comment—This is probably a good test item.

Example 5: (*correct answer)

	A	B	C	D
Frequency of responses	1*	1	6	32

Comment—The instructor may have indicated the wrong answer on the scoring sheet.

For more information on item analyses see Gronlund and Brookhart.[8(pp398–400)]

Writing Short-Answer and Essay Questions

A. These types of questions are easier to construct than multiple-choice questions.

B. They decrease the chance of correctly guessing because they require participants to think of the answers on their own.

C. They test higher level objectives where justification of ideas or explanation of thought process is required.

D. They can evaluate the affective domain by asking for opinions and values.

E. They are more difficult to correct and are open to subjectivity.

F. Practical ways to improve the reliability and objectivity of scoring include:

1. Have students put their name on the back of the exam (so evaluation is anonymous).

2. Delineate the criteria for grading each question.

3. Grade each individual question for all students before going to the next question.

4. Have 2 readers grade independently of knowing how the other person graded. Discuss discrepancies and work toward an agreement.

Oral Questioning

A. May use oral questions for formative assessment during the course of instruction or as part of a summative evaluation.

B. May be stand alone or part of another evaluation.

1. May be part of a clinical proficiency evaluation where students are asked questions about the procedure being performed.

2. May be useful when checking to be sure students can think on their feet.

C. Practical ways to improve the reliability and objectivity of scoring:

    1. Decide ahead of time what questions will be asked (students should be aware of the content areas to be addressed).

    2. Decide ahead of time what the criteria for scoring will be for the oral questions unless it is being used for feedback (formative).

    3. Train instructors who will be giving the evaluations for interrater reliability.

Portfolio Assessment

For real growth to occur, participants need to be involved with the evaluation process.

A. Portfolio assessment can take on various types of formats, depending on the purpose.

B. Portfolios can be a sampling of participants' work for the purpose of showing growth during a course, program, or an entire curriculum.

C. Portfolios can be used for formative evaluation, summative evaluation, or self-evaluation.

D. Consider the following questions when using the portfolio:

    1. What should go into the portfolio, and who should decide?

        • The instructors?

        • The students?

        • Both the instructor and students?

    2. Should it include everything that a student has done or a sampling of the work?

    3. How will the portfolio be assessed?

        • By the individual student or participant?

        • By the instructors?

        • By both the instructor and the students?

E. For more information on portfolios and for using rubrics for assessment, see Miller and colleagues,[7(pp288–312)] eHow,[9] and Portfolio Examples.[10]

Self-Evaluations

A. This is a process for individuals to reflect upon and document their own progress related to abilities, knowledge, skills, attitudes, and/or values.

    1. What have you learned?

    2. How have you used your new knowledge or skills?

    3. What do you still need to move forward?

    4. What are you doing differently because of this program?

B. This is an important lifelong skill.

C. Through self-evaluation, people can:

    1. Become aware of what they do well.

    2. Decide where they need to improve.

    3. Assess how they think and feel about their knowledge, skills, attitudes, and accomplishments.

    4. Make judgments about where they are in the learning process or in their development.

D. Self-evaluation is a skill to be learned and a process to be developed over time.

E. Participants often need guidance in learning the skill of self-evaluation.

F. For more information on self-evaluation, see Self-Evaluation Prompts[11] and Rolheiser and Ross.[12]

Writing and Using Clinical Evaluation Instruments

A. The evaluations should relate to the objectives for the course.

B. Critical incidents should be identified (i.e., the essential items that must be done satisfactorily to pass the evaluation independent of how well the student does overall).

C. The criteria to pass each evaluation should be clear.

D. There should be a place for the instructor to comment on areas related to strengths and areas where improvement is needed.

E. There should be a place for the student to write comments following the review of the evaluation.

F. There should be a place for the instructor and the student to sign and date the evaluation.

G. Train evaluators for interrater reliability.

Rating Scales

A. Rating scales are used to evaluate participants and for gathering information on program impacts and outcomes.

B. Scales can be used for evaluation of participants through observation.

C. Rating scale instruments can be used for self-evaluation or for evaluation by another person (family member, instructor, or group leader)

D. Often used for clinical evaluation.

E. Important considerations when writing rating scale evaluations:

1. Review learning outcomes and write rating scale to match.

2. Write descriptors for each number.

3. If it's a clinical evaluation, have a place for the students and instructor to sign and date.

4. Have a place for comments at the end.

5. If observation is being done, train the observers for interrater reliability.

6. Include a title and clear instructions.

F. A rating scale example is in Appendix B.

G. For more information on rating scales, see Miller and colleagues,[7(pp271–281)] Wisco Survey Power,[13] Gronlund and Brookhart,[9(pp114–115)] and HRIZONS.[14]

Likert Scales

A. A Likert scale is usually a self-report method of evaluation.

B. A Likert scale is useful to evaluate the affective domain or satisfaction levels.

C. Prepare a Likert scale using the delineated goals and objectives for the program.

D. This rating method usually has a 5-point scale (but can have more) and includes a neutral point.

E. Have the scale going in the same direction for each question.

F. If 5 is the best score, then it's easy to determine the most favorable total result.

G. An example of a Likert scale question is:
SD—Strongly disagree
D—Disagree
U—Undecided
A—Agree
SA—Strongly agree
You have the ability to develop a healthy meal plan for your family.

1	2	3	4	5
SD	D	U	A	SA

H. For more information on Likert scales, see Miller and colleagues[7(pp325–328)] and HRIZONS.[14]

Checklists

A. Checklists are used when the criterion of performance is just a *yes* or *no*.

B. The degree of performance is not being evaluated.

C. The behaviors being observed will come from the program outcomes.

D. A checklist may be part of a more comprehensive evaluation where a rating scale and oral questioning is included.

E. An example of a checklist question that is part of a clinical proficiency evaluation:

The student makes sound clinical judgments most of the time.   Yes   No

F. For more information on checklists, see Miller and colleagues[7(pp281–284)] and Gronlund and Brookhart.[13(pp119–120)]

Constraints Related to Evaluation

A. It may not be possible to perform a long-term evaluation.
   1. Financial resources not available.
   2. Program participants no longer accessible.

B. The number of participants responding to long-term evaluation may not be a large enough sample size to provide any valuable feedback regarding the program or its outcomes.

C. Time constraints may limit the number of formative assessments performed during the course of a program.

Questions

After reading this chapter on evaluation, go back and review Figure 1–1. Notice where formative and summative evaluation fits into the system. Also review the sample evaluation tools in Appendix B. They serve as examples for developing the evaluations for your learning unit or program.

1. Consider the program or unit of instruction that you are doing for your class project. Write down all the purposes of evaluations (both formative and summative).

2. What types of evaluations do you want to develop? (For example, multiple choice, short answers, essays, self-evaluations, checklists, rating scales, affective domain instruments, and/or others).

3. When your list is complete, match the purposes of each evaluation to the type of instrument you have chosen.

4. Develop the evaluation instruments. Describe any problems you are having with this assignment or any questions that occur to you.

5. Describe what steps you have taken to assure validity of your evaluation instruments.

6. Describe how you will assure reliability of the evaluation results.

7. When will you give participants the formative evaluations and how will you use the results?

8. When will you give participants the summative evaluations and how will you use the results?

Practice Cases

Here are the 3 cases you worked on in the previous chapters. This time, design the evaluations that you would use for each case. Include all the formative and summative evaluations you would need to use. Review your goals, standards, and objectives to be sure they are all covered in the evaluation system.

Case 1: Healthcare Clinic

You are an employee in a healthcare clinic. Your supervisor has asked you to create a program to decrease the risk of H1N1 flu in current employees and patients who visit the clinic.

Case 2: After School Program

You volunteer at an after school program for children in grades 3 through 5. Currently, they complete their homework, participate in craft projects, and have a snack. You think it might be a good idea to add physical activity and a nutrition component to the existing program. Your supervisor agrees and asks you to develop a proposal for this.

Case 3: Pharmacy

You are an intern at a local pharmacy. Many clients come in to ask questions of the pharmacists about preventing the onset of certain diseases. You realize it would be a good idea to have a series of wellness lectures about obesity, diabetes, cardiovascular disease, and hypertension. Your supervisor says that this will be a great program for you to develop.

References

1. Timmreck TC. *Planning, Program Development, and Evaluation. A Handbook for Health Promotion, Aging & Health Service.* Sudbury, MA: Jones and Bartlett; 2003.
2. Hodges BC. *Assessment and Planning in Health Programs.* Sudbury, MA: Jones and Bartlett; 2005.
3. McKenzie JF, Neiger BL, Thackeray R. *Planning, Implementing, and Evaluating Health Promotion Programs.* San Francisco, CA: Pearson Education, Inc; 2009.
4. Hayden J, ed. *The Health Education Specialist: A Study Guide for Professional Competence.* 4th ed. Whitehall, PA: The National Commission for Health Educational Credentialing, Inc; 2000.
5. Davis BG. *Tools for Teaching.* 2nd ed. San Francisco, CA: Jossey-Bass; 2009.
6. Cuseo J. *The One-Minute Paper.* http://www.oncourseworkshop.com/Awareness012.htm. Accessed March 15, 2010.
7. Miller MD, Linn RL, Gronlund NE. *Measurement and Assessment in Teaching.* Boston, MA: Allyn & Bacon; 2009.
8. Gronlund NE, Brookhart SM. *Writing Instructional Objectives.* 8th ed. Upper Saddle River, NJ: Pearson Education; 2009.
9. eHow. *How to Do Just About Anything—How to Make a Portfolio.* http://www.ehow.com/how_2046018_make-portfolio.html. Accessed March 15, 2009.
10. *Portfolio Examples.* http://www.dartmouth.edu/~csrc/students/portfolio/examples/index.html. Accessed March 15, 2009.
11. *Self-Evaluation Prompts.* http://www.evergreen.edu/washcenter/resources/acl/e3.html. Accessed March 15, 2010.
12. Rolheiser C, Ross JA. *Student Self-Evaluation: What Research Says and What Practice Shows.* http://www.cdl.org/resource-library/articles/self_eval.php. Accessed March 15, 2010.
13. *Wisco Survey Power. Create, Collect and Analyze Surveys and Web Forms. Wisco Survey—Numeric Rating Scale Survey Questions.* http://www.wiscosurvey.com/webhelp/numeric-rating-scale.htm. Accessed March 15, 2010.
14. HRIZONS. *Use the Right Rating Scale for Your Performance Reviews.* http://hrizons.com/wordpress/?p=37. Assessed March 15, 2010.

A

Needs Assessment Instruments

Introduction

Needs assessment forms found in the following pages are examples. You may use them to get ideas or as models for developing your own assessment forms. The needs assessment examples include:

Form 1. Survey: This is an example of a survey that can be used to assess the needs and interests of a group at the beginning of a course or seminar. Although the goals of a course are usually set prior to meeting the group for the first time, modifications can be made to address the needs of the specific audience.

Form 2. Questionnaire: This questionnaire is an example of one that could be given to participants preparing for an exercise program to help the rehabilitation team assist the clients with their exercise plans. A sample number of responses to each question is included to help you begin to think about how one might use the results for a group program. Consider that there are 8 people in the group.

Form 3. Focus Group: The needs assessment was designed for a needs assessment focus group to gather information from parents who have children with diabetes. The purpose is to learn about the experiences they have had with the healthcare system as they take care of their children.

Form 4. Observation: The observational instrument was designed to gather information to design a bicycle safety course for high school students in an urban community. There will be a training session for the observers to assure they are looking for the same behaviors. The training will help to improve interrater reliability of the data collection.

Form 5. Interview: This interview was designed to gather information from teachers about their perceptions of health literacy in the 3rd grade and to determine what might work in their school. Their responses will provide information about possibilities and to decide what other needs assessment strategies might be helpful in planning the program.

Form 6. Survey: This needs assessment survey was designed to gather information for an osteoporosis education and prevention program for mothers and daughters. This was designed to be part of a wellness program held in a pharmacy.

Form 7. Multiple Needs Assessments for One Program: A variety of needs assessment strategies were used to develop an asthma pilot project to address the educational needs of Latino families. A sampling of data used to develop this program is included. This project was funded by HRSA Bureau of Health Professions with support from the Institute on Urban Health Research, Northeastern University. This example is used to show the range of needs assessment strategies that were used for one program.

Needs Assessment for Course or Program

After reviewing the course syllabus, textbook and/or materials for this course, please respond to the following questions:

1. What do you hope to accomplish in this course?

2. How well do you think this course will fulfill your needs and goals?

3. Is there anything that you would like to have covered in the course that doesn't appear on the syllabus?

4. What do you look forward to the most in this class?

5. What learning strategies have worked best for you in the past? (You may find it helpful to do one of the learning styles inventories available on the Internet).

6. Do you have any concerns up to this point about the class? If so, please describe.

7. Is there anything you would like to tell the instructors that has not been addressed in this survey?

Needs Assessment for a Group Exercise Program

This questionnaire is to help us design an exercise program that best suits you. We want you to develop a program that you can do for a long time and will help you have a healthy lifestyle. Please circle your responses. **Note:** A sample number of responses have been included. These can be helpful in discussing how to use survey results to plan programs.

1. Have you exercised regularly (more than 2 times per week) during the past 2 years?

    yes—3   no—5

2. Which of the following factors do (or would) motivate you to exercise?

    a. Gives me a great start to the day—3

    b. I have heard it gives one more energy—5

    c. Exercising with others—5

    d. Help me live longer—8

    e. Information about what I should be doing—6

    f. Learn how to use equipment correctly—7

3. What do you consider the barriers for you in exercising at least 3 times per week?

    a. Laziness—3

    b. The weather, especially if cold and rainy—6

    c. Afraid of having another heart attack—7

    d. I get bored while exercising—3

    e. I just don't know what I can do, especially since my heart attack—6

4. Indicate which of the following exercises you are most likely to do on a regular basis. (Choose all that apply.)

    a. Walking or jogging on a track—8

    b. Walking on a treadmill—7

    c. Elliptical machine—2

    d. StairMaster—0

    e. Bicycle—5

    In addition, 6 people indicated that they did not know what the elliptical machine was; 5 didn't know about the StairMaster.

5. What are your goals for going through this 6-week program? (Choose all that apply and add anything else important to you)

    a. Prevent another heart attack—8

    b. Lose weight—7

    c. Be healthier overall—8

    d. Learn how to quit smoking—1

    e. Control blood pressure—6

    Other responses: make new friends who understand what I have gone through—6; hoping to learn about healthy foods—5

6. Do you have any questions or concerns that were not addressed on this survey?

(Note to students: Remember these data represent sample responses. Consider how you would use results for a group program. N = 8)

Focus Group for Diabetic Education Program

You have been selected to participate in a focus group because of your successful experience caring for a child with diabetes. Your responses will help us to design a program for parents of newly diagnosed children. Our goal is to assist them in working successfully within the healthcare system. There will be two interviewers present. One will take notes and the other will ask the questions. With your permission, the interviewers will use a tape recorder. The session will last for 90 minutes. Thank you for your help! Your participation is very much appreciated.

Focus Group Questions:

1. Please describe your experience or having a child with diabetes.

2. What does success in caring for your diabetic child mean to you?

3. What strategies have contributed to your success in caring for your child?

4. In what ways has the healthcare system helped you and your child?

5. In what ways do you feel your needs have not been met?

6. What healthcare professionals have helped the most and in what ways?

7. How did you find the answers to your questions related to diabetes?

8. If you were to now repeat the process of learning to care for your child from the time of diagnosis, what would you do differently?

9. What advice would you give to parents with a newly diagnosed child?

10. Is there anything else you would like to say or ask before we end this session?

Observational Needs Assessment of
Bicycle Safety Behavior in an Urban Area

This observation sheet has been created in order to observe the behavior of urban bicyclists and their actions as it complies with Chapter 85 Section 11B of the Massachusetts Bicycle Law, and general safety guidelines identified by the Massachusetts Bicycle Coalition.

Name of observer _____

Date of observation _____

Total number of bicyclists observed_____

Time observation began _____ Time observation concluded _____

Neighborhood/district observed _____

Location of observer: (*cross streets, address, etc.*)

_____

_____

_____

_____

Period of observation

*Sunrise*_____ *Morning*_____ *Afternoon*_____ *Sunset*_____ *Evening*_____

Type of bicycle

Street (thin wheeled)..Yes (*Number observed*)_____ or No

Terrain (thick wheeled)..Yes (*Number observed*)_____ or No

Hybrid bicycle (thin frame, thick wheel).............................Yes (*Number observed*)_____ or No

Observations pertaining to the bicycle operator

1. **Is riding single file on any bikeway.**

   Yes (*Number observed*) _____ No (*Number observed*)_____ Not observed

2. **Gives audible warning (when possible) when changing direction or course.**

   Yes (*Number observed*) _____ No (*Number observed*)_____ Not observed

3. **Has parked bicycle in a manner that does not obstruct traffic—neither pedestrian nor vehicular.**

   Yes (*Number observed*) _____ No (*Number observed*)_____ Not observed

4. **Has one hand on the handlebars at all times.**

   Yes (*Number observed*) _____ No (*Number observed*)_____ Not observed

5. Is not carrying a package or bundle in any way other than in a basket, on a rack, or towing behind the bicycle.

   Yes (*Number observed*) _____ No (*Number observed*)_____ Not observed

6. Has a reflector visible on each of the pedals, and is noticeable from sunset to sunrise hours.

   Yes (*Number observed*) _____ No (*Number observed*)_____ Not observed

7. Is driving on appropriate bikeway—road, shoulder, or designated bike lane.

   Yes (*Number observed*) _____ No (*Number observed*)_____ Not observed

8. Passes cars on the right, only.

   Yes (*Number observed*) _____ No (*Number observed*)_____ Not observed

9. Is obeying all traffic rules and regulations.

   Yes (*Number observed*) _____ No (*Number observed*)_____ Not observed

10. Gives pedestrians the right of way.

    Yes (*Number observed*) _____ No (*Number observed*)_____ Not observed

11. Obeys traffic lights and signs.

    Yes (*Number observed*) _____ No (*Number observed*)_____ Not observed

12. Is wearing protective and secured head gear, such as a helmet.

    Yes (*Number observed*) _____ No (*Number observed*)_____ Not observed

Additional observations: Please note anything else you observed during this process.

_____

_____

_____

_____

_____

_____

_____

_____

Courtesy of Andrew R. Taylor

Needs Assessment for Health Literacy Program

This interview was created to gather information from elementary school teachers about the usefulness of developing comprehensive health literacy education in the classroom. The process of the interview will be one on one with all 3rd grade teachers at a specified elementary school.

1. How do you define health literacy?

2. How would you describe the basic literacy skills of your students?

3. What are the characteristics of the high-performing students versus the lower performing students?

4. What do you believe are the strengths of this school's ability to teach health literacy?

5. What are the weaknesses of this school's ability to teach health literacy?

6. What motivates your students to participate in the classroom?

7. What do you believe are the biggest health risks facing children in your grade level?

8. What topics related to health are taught in the classroom?

9. Would you be interested in teaching a more comprehensive health curriculum?

10. What do you perceive as obstacles to teaching a comprehensive health curriculum?

11. Are you aware of any literature about health written for elementary age children?

12. What resources would you need to teach health education in the classroom?

13. What is a realistic way to assess students understanding of health information?

14. Is there anything else you want to say that I didn't ask you during this interview?

Courtesy of Andrew R. Taylor

Across Generations:
Osteoporosis Education and Prevention Program

Needs assessment survey: Your responses to the following questions will help me design a program that incorporates educational needs and questions that you have about osteoporosis.

1. Please list all the risk factors that you know about for osteoporosis.

2. Please indicate your level of personal concern regarding osteoporosis.

1	2	3	4	5
No concern	Somewhat concerned	Not sure	Concerned	Very concerned

3. Please rate your calcium intake.

1	2	3	4	5
Poor	Sometimes okay	Adequate	Good	Excellent

4. Please estimate the time spent engaging in physical activity per week.

5. What activities make up the time indicated above?

6. Would you be interested in attending a mother/daughter program on osteoporosis education and prevention?

7. What time of day would be best for you to attend the program?

8. If so, what specific questions or concerns would you like addressed?

Thank you for taking the time to answer this survey. The program schedule will be posted in the pharmacy at least 2 weeks in advance. If you would like information about the schedule sent in an email, please write your email address here:

Courtesy of Stephanie N. Giangreco

Form 7

Needs Assessment: Asthma Education Program Plan[1]

1. Sampling of data supporting the need:
   a. 15 million people in United States (1998) reported they were diagnosed with asthma (5 million under age of 18)[2]
   b. Asthma listed as cause of death in approximately 5500 people (out of 2.3 million deaths)[2]
   c. 474,000 asthma hospitalizations[2]
   d. 11.9 million medical visits[2]
   e. Groups affected vary with race, ethnicity and urban location.
      • Higher in poor urban communities
      • Higher among African Americans—prevalence in 2002 was 9.3%[3]
      • Higher in Puerto Rico—prevalence 11.5%[3]
      • Overall prevalence—7.5%[3]
      • Underreported in both groups[2,3]
   f. Prevalence in children
      • A leading serious cause of illness among children (in 2001 affected 6.3 million, accounting for 728,000 emergency room visits and 214,000 hospitalizations)[3]
      • The most common chronic illness affecting Hispanic/Puerto Rican children.[4]
      • Hispanic/Puerto Rican children had the highest asthma prevalence (48.6%) followed by African American children (35%).[5]
      • Hispanic/Puerto Rican children also have the most severe asthma in comparison.
      • Hispanic/Puerto Rican children's asthma severity was also greater than that in African American children.[5]
      • There is a marked increase in risk for asthma in children of Hispanic mothers that is not explained by SES, material age, or environmental exposure of tobacco.[6]
      • Hispanic/Puerto Rican children are more likely to live in urban areas with poor housing conditions. Therefore, there is an increase risk exposure to certain indoor allergens among these children.[4]
      • Hispanic/Puerto Ricans are more likely to have low literacy and lack of knowledge about asthma, preventative therapy, symptoms, medications, and delays in obtaining healthcare services. They are more likely to lack insurance coverage for medications, equipment, and doctor visits.[4]

2. Expert input from Northeastern University faculty multidisciplinary advisory board contributed to the study design, protocols, and curriculum materials. Representatives were from counseling psychology, nursing, pharmacy, physical therapy, respiratory therapy, and the physician assistant program.

3. Focus groups were conducted with Latino families having children with asthma. The purpose was to determine what real issues the families were dealing with and what they needed in a program.

4. Testimonials were based on in-depth interviews with 3 Latino parents who have children with asthma. The purpose was to thoroughly explore the issues faced by Latino parents of children with asthma.

5. Based on the needs assessment, the curriculum was developed in Spanish and then translated into English and provided in both languages.

References

1. Amaro H, Watson M. A pilot study of an asthma psychol-educational intervention for Latino families. Unpublished. 2003.
2. Institutes of Medicine. Committee on the Assessment of Asthma and Indoor Air, Division of Health Promotion and Disease Prevention. *Clearing the Air: Asthma and Indoor Exposures*. Washington, DC: National Academy Press; 2000. http://www.nap.edu/openbook.php?record_id=9610&page=1. Accessed March 23, 2010.
3. Centers for Disease Control and Prevention. 2004. http://www.cdc.gov/health/asthma.
4. Lara M, Morgenstern H, Duan N, Brook RH. Elevated asthma morbidity in Puerto Rican children: A review of possible risk and prognostic factors. *West J Med*. 1999;170(2):75–84.
5. Clouthier MM, Wakefield DB, Hall CB, Bailit HL. Childhood asthma in an urban community. *Chest*. 2002;1571–1579.
6. Litonjua AA, Carey VJ, Weiss ST, Gold DR. Socioeconomic factors and residence are associated with asthma prevalence. *Pediatr Pulmonol*. 1999;28:394–401.

APPENDIX

B

Sample Evaluation Instruments

Introduction

The evaluation forms found in the following pages are examples. You may use them to get ideas or as models for developing your own evaluations. The evaluations include:

Form 1. Rating Scale: This is an evaluation developed by Leah MacPherson, a professor of dental hygiene. This form can be used for evaluation by peers, self, or the instructor. Each number on the scale has a descriptor so that students are aware of how they will be rated in each area. The course syllabus gives students further information about the conditions under which they must repeat the evaluation; for example, if a student receives a potentially ineffective or lower rating. Having a place for recommendations gives students further descriptive feedback. A place for the student signature indicates the importance of assuring that the student reviews the evaluation.

Form 2. Affective Domain: This is an example of an affective domain formative evaluation, developed by Andrew R. Taylor. This form can be used for self-evaluation, peer evaluation, or evaluation by the instructor. The scale is a continuum with the lowest and highest ratings delineated. The evaluation is for formative feedback to the participant with the goal of seeing progress over time.

Form 3. Self-Evaluation: This is a self-evaluation form developed to help students prepare for presentations. Students are asked questions about what they want to accomplish in the presentation and the effective presentation skills that they would like to demonstrate. They choose 3 skills they want to be evaluated on during the presentation. The concept is that by working on just 3 skills, other skills improve as as well. After the presentation, students self-evaluate how well they accomplished the objectives and how well they demonstrated effective presentation skills. Their self-evaluation is included as part of the total evaluation.

Form 4. Likert Scale Survey: This is a long-term, follow-up survey to determine how well practitioners incorporated information from a continuing education course. The effectiveness of the delivery of such a program is measured at the end of the program. However, the long-term outcome of the program effectiveness is measured after participants have utilized the information.

Forms 5 and 6 Surveys: These are evaluation forms designed for an Alzheimer's Day program developed by Laura Desrochers and Andrew R. Taylor. Form 5 was designed to be used at the completion of the program, and Form 6 was designed for a summative long-term evaluation to be given 3–6 months after the program.

Form 7 Survey: This is an example of an evaluation that incorporates all 3 domains of learning: the cognitive, affective, and psychomotor domains. This evaluation was developed by Marianne O'Shea to be used when teaching oral hygiene skills.

Instrumental Lab for Dental Hygienists

Clinician:_____   Evaluator: Peer   Self   Instructor

Evaluator:_____   Feedback Session: 1   2   3

Date:_____

Directions—Please evaluate each criterion and circle the appropriate number.

4—Demonstrates skill completely, accurately, consistently, and correctly.
3—Demonstrates skill with minor errors.
2—Demonstrates skill inconsistently or with major errors.
1—Unable to demonstrate skill.

Objectives	Evaluation	Comments
1. Uses correct working end.	4 3 2 1	
2. Keeps terminal shank parallel to the long axis of the tooth.	4 3 2 1	
3. Adapts tip to the tooth.	4 3 2 1	
4. Rolls handle to maintain adaption.	4 3 2 1	
5. Uses effective exploring stroke: good length, control, and overlapping stroke.	4 3 2 1	
6. Demonstrates correct stroke: oblique, horizontal, and vertical.	4 3 2 1	
7. Extends tip interproximally.	4 3 2 1	
8. Uses all criteria for patient/operator positioning.	4 3 2 1	
9. Uses all criteria for grasp.	4 3 2 1	
10. Uses all criteria for finger rests and uses extra-/intraoral fulcrums.	4 3 2 1	
11. Uses all criteria for mouth mirror.	4 3 2 1	
12. Uses correct hand/finger position; pivots, rotates, and uses wrist rock motion.	4 3 2 1	

Overall performance: Total score _____   Recommendations:
Highly effective   45–48
Effective   31–44
Potentially ineffective   16–30
Ineffective   12–15

Student comments:

Student signature _____   Date_____

Evaluator signature_____   Date_____

Courtesy of Leah MacPherson

Form 2

Affective Domain Role-Play Evaluation

The following form will be used to assist students in developing effective interaction skills while solving problems in a role-play format. This form should be used as a standard evaluation for each role-play and may be used for self-evaluation, peer evaluation, or feedback from the instructor during the process of learning. Remember there is no such thing as a perfect role-play. The goal is for participants to see progress over time.

An *X* is to be marked on each continuum at the point that best indicates the participant's performance. A comment should also be included to provide each participant with suggestions for improvement. 1 = Needs improvement   4 = Highest quality

Introduction	1	2	3	4

Comments: _____

Confirmation **inquiry or conflict**	1	2	3	4

Comments: _____

Eye contact **and temperament**	1	2	3	4

Comments: _____

Character **management**	1	2	3	4

Comments: _____

Commitment to **role-play**	1	2	3	4

Comments: _____

Persistence to **resolution**	1	2	3	4

Comments: _____

Overall quality	1	2	3	4

Comments: _____

Participant signature: _____   Date_____

Peer or instructor signature:_____   Date: _____

Courtesy of Andrew R. Taylor

Self-Evaluation of Class Presentation

Name: _____ Date: _____

Presentation title: _____

Directions

Please complete questions 1–6 in preparation for your presentation. The questions are designed to help you focus on what you will cover and the effective presentation skills that you want to demonstrate. Questions 7–9 are designed to help you process your performance and should be filled out after the presentation. You will then submit this form to the instructor for feedback.

1. What part of your presentation is the most interesting to you?

2. List the important points you would like to share with the group.

3. What are your objectives for the presentation?

4. What strategies will you use? How will your strategies reach participants with different learning styles?

5. What materials did you develop for the presentation? How do you rate their quality?

6. Circle 3 skills that you want to demonstrate during your presentation.

Eye contact	No fidgeting	No reading of slides	Rate of speech
Confidence	No distractors	Tone and volume	Good posture
Appropriate hand gestures	Clarity	Knowledge	Other_____

Please answer the following questions after your presentation.

7. How well did you meet your objectives and cover the content?

8. How well did you demonstrate effective presentation skills (with emphasis on the 3 you chose)?

9. If you had it to do over again, what would you do differently to improve the quality of your presentation?

Form 4

Teaching Health Professionals
Tobacco Cessation Interventions

Please help us assess the effectiveness of the tobacco cessation interventions course you participated in 6 months ago. This survey is to determine how much you have incorporated into your professional practice. Your responses will help us to improve future courses in the area of smoking cessation interventions. Thank you for your help!

1. Please rate how well you have incorporated the smoking cessation program into your professional practice.

1	2	3	4	5
Very well	Well	Moderately well	Not very well	Not at all

Comments:

2. How valuable was the program in helping you to become a tobacco cessation intervention specialist?

1	2	3	4	5
Most valuable	Valuable	Moderately valuable	Slightly valuable	Not at all

Comments:

3. Would you recommend this program to a colleague?

1	2	3
Definitely	Not sure	No

Comments:

4. Please describe how you have incorporated smoking cessation into your practice.

5. Do you have any suggestions that would help us to design a more helpful program?

Again, thank you for your input.

Alzheimer's Day Program

Evaluation

We really appreciate your participation in our program. Please take a few minutes to help us evaluate how we did. This evaluation is to be completed at the conclusion of the program.

1. What is the first word or thought that comes to mind when thinking about the program you participated in today? Why that word or phrase?

2. Which of the parts within our program were most effective for you?

3. What did you find most useful about the information shared?

4. What aspect of our program have we done best?

5. What could we do to improve our program?

6. What advice would you give future participants in our program?

7. Would you recommend this program for other caregivers?

8. Would you be interested in a continuation of this program?

Please rate how satisfied you were with the following parts of our program.

Provided materials (pamphlets, literature, pretest, course packet)

Not at all satisfied	Somewhat satisfied	Neutral	Satisfied	Very satisfied

Learning strategies (group discussion, role-play, site visitation, guest speakers)

Not at all satisfied	Somewhat satisfied	Neutral	Satisfied	Very satisfied

Presenters' skills and knowledge (Laura Desrochers and Drew Taylor)

Not at all satisfied	Somewhat satisfied	Neutral	Satisfied	Very satisfied

Additional comments?

Thank you very much for your participation!

Courtesy of Laura Desrochers and Andrew R. Taylor

Form 6

Alzheimer's Day Programs

Thank you for participating in the Alzheimer's Day program. We hope that you have been successful in using the knowledge gained from the program. This survey is for us to determine how successful we were in assisting you. Your responses will help us improve the program. Thank you very much for your assistance with this.

Evaluation of Progression

This evaluation is to be completed between 3 and 6 months after attending program.

1. In the last 3–6 months, how many times has your patient or loved one been hospitalized?

2. How many of these hospitalizations have been due to an accident related to care such as falling or inappropriate dosage of medications?

3. Are you in touch with an appropriate specialist regarding the care of your Alzheimer's patient or loved one?

4. Are you utilizing any alternative services for your patient or loved one? Explain.

5. How has your routine care changed since attending our program?

6. Have you noticed a change in your patient or loved one's behavior and demeanor since implementing a change? Explain.

7. How is your relationship with your patient or loved one different since implementing changes in their services or routines?

8. Have you felt a change in stress level, either an increase or a decrease, resulting from changes in routine or behavior?

9. Please write any comments or suggestions you have that will help make our program better in the future.

Thank you again!

Courtesy of Laura Desrochers and Andrew R. Taylor

Oral Health Evaluation

Participant name: _____ Clinician name: _____

Date: _____

There are 3 parts to this evaluation (cognitive, affective, and psychomotor domains). The participant will be evaluated at the end of the session. If a participant does not demonstrate skills at the acceptable level, a review will be done in the areas that need reinforcement.

Cognitive knowledge: The participant will be asked the following questions to assess the knowledge gained from the individual oral health information session:

1. Why is oral health important to your overall health?

2. Name 3 ways in which you can improve your oral health.

3. Where can you go to receive oral health care?

Overall cognitive performance: (Circle the score)

   1 question correct = poor understanding

   1.5–2 questions correct = fair understanding

   2.5 questions correct = good understanding (*acceptable performance)

   3 questions correct = excellent understanding

Cognitive performance: If the participant does not receive a 3 in each area, information about the importance of oral hygiene will be reinforced.

Comments:

Affective skills: On a continuum, mark the point that best describes the participant performance:

   1 = Poor, does not meet expectations

   2 = Fair, barely meets expectations

   3 = Good, meets expectations (*acceptable performance)

   4 = Exceeds expectations

1. The participant is willing to actively attend the single oral health information session.

   1   2   3   4

2. The participant is engaged in the information session by asking questions.

   1   2   3   4

3. The participant is pursuing an improvement in his or her oral health by obtaining referrals to preventative oral health services.

   1   2   3   4

Affective performance: If the participant does not receive a 3 in each area, information about the importance of oral hygiene will be reinforced.

Comments:

Psychomotor skills: This evaluation involves a demonstration of brushing and flossing.

Evaluate each criterion and circle the appropriate number:

    1 = Unable to demonstrate skill

    2 = Demonstrates skill inconsistently or with major errors

    3 = Demonstrates skill with minor errors

    4 = Demonstrates skill completely, accurately, and correctly

Brushing

Skill	Evaluation	Comments
1. Places the toothbrush at a 45° angle to the gums	1 2 3 4	
2. Moves the brush back and forth gently in short strokes	1 2 3 4	
3. Brushes the outer surfaces, the inside surfaces and the chewing surfaces of all teeth	1 2 3 4	
4. Cleans the inside surface of the front teeth, tilts the brush vertically and makes several up and down strokes	1 2 3 4	
5. Brushes the tongue to remove bacteria	1 2 3 4	

Flossing

Skill	Evaluation	Comments
1. Uses about 18 inches of floss wound around one of the middle fingers, with the rest wound around the opposite middle finger	1 2 3 4	
2. Holds the floss tightly between the thumbs and forefingers and gently inserts it between the teeth	1 2 3 4	
3. Curves the floss into a *C* shape against the side of the tooth	1 2 3 4	
4. Rubs the floss gently up and down, keeping it pressed against the tooth; doesn't jerk or snap the floss	1 2 3 4	
5. Flosses all the teeth, including back teeth	1 2 3 4	